MARIE STOPES was born on 15 October 1880 in Edinburgh, the elder daughter of Henry Stopes and Charlotte Carmichael Stopes. She was educated in Scotland until 1894 when her parents moved to London. She attended North London Collegiate School and then University College London, from which she graduated in 1902 with honours in both botany and geology. In 1904 she obtained her Ph.D. at the University of Munich and there met a Japanese botanist, Kenjiro Fujii, with whom she fell in love. In 1905 she was awarded her D.Sc.—the youngest woman to be awarded the degree—and was to become a distinguished palaeobotanist. From 1904 until 1910 she taught at the University of Manchester, though in 1907 she was given leave to do research in Japan. It was during this trip that the relationship with Fujii finally ended. In 1910 she left Manchester and went to Canada to study carboniferous flora. In December 1910 she met and then married a Canadian geneticist, Reginald Ruggles Gates. The two returned to England in 1911. The marriage was deeply unhappy and as a result of her efforts to extricate herself from it she began to write the first drafts of what was to become *Married Love*—an attack on marriage as it was and a guide to what it could become. *Married Love* was published in March 1918 and was hugely successful, both in Britain and abroad, as was its successor *Wise Parenthood* (1918), a birth-control manual. In 1918 Stopes married Humphrey Verdon Roe, who had partly financed the publication of *Married Love*, and together they became increasingly involved in the birth-control movement. In 1921 they founded the Holloway Clinic, the first birth-control clinic in Britain, and the Society for Constructive Birth Control. Stopes became an ever more controversial and publicity-conscious figure who alienated many in the birth-control movement, though a tireless and successful proponent of the cause. She wrote voluminously, not just on marriage and sexuality, but plays, novels, poetry, film scripts, and children's stories. As she got older and more difficult to work with, she tended to withdraw into literature, though she was very much less successful as a literary figure than she was as a scientist. By the late 1930s her marriage to Verdon Roe was more or less over and they largely lived apart until his death in 1949. She outlived him by nine years, dying on 2 October 1958.

ROSS MCKIBBIN is Fellow and Tutor in Modern History at St John's College, Oxford. His previous publications include *The Evolution of the Labour Party 1910–1924*, *The Ideologies of Class*, and *Classes and Cultures: England 1918–1951*.

OXFORD WORLD'S CLASSICS

MARIE STOPES

Married Love

Edited with an Introduction and Notes by
ROSS McKIBBIN

OXFORD
UNIVERSITY PRESS

OXFORD
UNIVERSITY PRESS

Great Clarendon Street, Oxford OX2 6DP

Oxford University Press is a department of the University of Oxford.
It furthers the University's objective of excellence in research, scholarship,
and education by publishing worldwide in

Oxford New York

Auckland Bangkok Buenos Aires Cape Town Chennai
Dar es Salaam Delhi Hong Kong Istanbul Karachi Kolkata
Kuala Lumpur Madrid Melbourne Mexico City Mumbai Nairobi
São Paulo Shanghai Taipei Tokyo Toronto

Oxford is a registered trade mark of Oxford University Press
in the UK and in certain other countries

Published in the United States
by Oxford University Press Inc., New York

Copyright © The Galton Institute
Editorial material © Ross McKibbin 2004

The moral rights of the author have been asserted

Database right Oxford University Press (maker)

First published as an Oxford World's Classics paperback 2004

British Library Cataloguing in Publication Data

Data available

Library of Congress Cataloging-in-Publication Data
Stopes, Marie Carmichael, 1880–1958.
Married love/Marie Stopes ; edited with an introduction
and notes by Ross McKibbin.
p. cm.—(Oxford world's classics)
Includes bibliographical references and index.
1. Marriage.   I. McKibbin, Ross.   II. Title.   III. Oxford world's classics
(Oxford University Press)

HQ734.S887 2004
306.872—dc22   2004041593

ISBN 0-19-280432-4

1

Typeset in Ehrhardt
by RefineCatch Limited, Bungay, Suffolk
Printed in Great Britain by
Clays Ltd, St Ives plc

CONTENTS

ACKNOWLEDGEMENTS

A NUMBER of people are party to the preparation of this book. I would like to thank Mary Hilton for encouragement and sensible advice, and Dr Lesley A. Hall and Brother J. Hodkinson SJ for the friendliness and speed with which they answered my queries. I must thank especially Janet Howarth and Judith Luna, who read the manuscript and who commented on it helpfully and patiently. The remaining faults are, of course, mine.

R.McK.

INTRODUCTION

MANY writers hope that what they write will have profound cultural and social significance. Only a few, however, know that it will. Marie Stopes[1] was one. On 6 July 1915 she told Margaret Sanger, the American birth-control pioneer, that she was finishing a book 'which will probably electrify this country'.[2] That book, which was to be called *Married Love* and was published in March 1918, did indeed electrify the country. This is the thirtieth English edition; and that figure, of course, excludes American editions and the fourteen foreign-language translations. For Stopes, it began a career of remarkable celebrity; although, as we shall see, *Married Love* differs in some important respects from her later writing and sexual politics.

Marie Stopes before Married Love

Marie Carmichael Stopes was born in Edinburgh on 15 October 1880, the elder daughter of Charlotte Carmichael (1841–1929) and Henry Stopes (1852–1902), and died on 2 October 1958. Charlotte Carmichael was a formidable, severe, though not unloving mother. She was Scottish and a member of the Free Church: the strongly Protestant atmosphere of Stopes's upbringing was something she remembered without pleasure. Her mother was what once would have been called a bluestocking: a major Shakespearian scholar, an

[1] There are several Stopeses in this introduction. Marie Stopes will throughout be known as Stopes. Her parents will be given their full names.

[2] Quoted in Richard A. Soloway, 'The Galton Lecture 1996: Marie Stopes, Eugenics and the Birth Control Movement', in R. A. Peel (ed.), *Marie Stopes, Eugenics and the English Birth Control Movement* (London, 1997), 49. Margaret Sanger (1879–1966), perhaps the most influential figure in the international birth-control movement, was trained as a nurse and, as a result of her nursing experience in New York, became convinced that birth control was necessary for the prosperity and health of working-class women. In 1914 she founded the *Woman Rebel*. As a result of her advocacy there of birth control she was prosecuted for obscenity. She went to England in 1915, partly to escape conviction, and met Stopes. In 1916 she established the first American birth-control clinic, and in 1921 the American Birth Control League, later the Planned Parenthood Federation. Although once allies, Sanger and Stopes eventually separated, largely because Stopes could not cede equality, leave alone primacy, to anyone else in the birth-control movement. See also p. 115, note to p. 88.

important and innovative writer of a feminist history and political theory,[3] exceptionally knowledgeable on many things. She was also very political: a suffragette, an active proponent of rational dress for women,[4] more unusually, an opponent of smoking.[5] As Stopes got older her mother became more remote, literally as well as figuratively. Although dutiful enough when the girls were young, she was inclined to regard motherhood as an impediment to her career as lecturer and scholar. As she resumed that career she increasingly spent less time at home: so adding a physical to an emotional distance from her children.

Marie's father, Henry Stopes, was from a well-to-do Colchester brewing family and was himself an engineer and architect of brew houses and brewing technology. What primarily interested him, however, was palaeontology and archaeology, and, though in a sense an amateur, he was a distinguished palaeontologist who made the Swanscombe shale quarries famous.[6] Henry Stopes was eleven years younger than his wife, though not unlike her in character and intellectual interests. They had first met at a meeting of the British Association—Stopes said she was a child of the British Association—and both shared the Association's intellectual seriousness and progressive-mindedness. Of Quaker origin, Henry Stopes had become an active Congregationalist (an unusual religion for a brewer) and that tended to reinforce his wife's Free Church Presbyterianism. The marriage, though not exactly a failure, was not exactly a success, and sexual incompatibility was largely the reason. Charlotte clearly found sexual relations difficult and distasteful. To the extent that the marriage had passion it was all Henry's. As he lay dying, Charlotte noted 'that the sensual look has passed away from your face that so pained me'.[7] Henry tried several times to resuscitate the marriage but eventually abandoned the attempt; both husband

---

[3] See here, e.g. C. Carmichael Stopes, *British Freewomen: Their Historical Privilege* (London, 1894); *The Sphere of 'Man' in relation to that of 'Woman' in the Constitution* (London, 1907).

[4] She even wrote 'a bright, piquant article' on rational dress (at Oscar Wilde's request) for *The Woman's World*, of which Wilde was for a time literary editor (J. Rose, *Marie Stopes and the Sexual Revolution* (London, 1992), 10).

[5] See *Woman's Herald*, 15 Aug. 1891. I am grateful to Mrs Janet Howarth for this reference.

[6] For her father's career as archaeologist and palaeontologist see K. Briant, *Marie Stopes: A Biography* (London, 1962), 28–9.

[7] Quoted in R. Hall, *Marie Stopes: A Biography* (London, 1977), 19.

and wife thereafter went their own way.[8] As far as his absences permitted, Stopes was close to her father. She enjoyed his company, especially digging and excavating with him, and he was very protective, indeed too protective, of her.

It is tempting to see in the parents the influences which shape the character of the child. In Stopes's case this takes us only so far. Intellectually, she was certainly influenced by her parents: her feminism, the commitment to rational dress, the conviction that women must have vocations outside childbearing, the way she educated her own son—all these she must, at least partly, have owed to her mother.[9] It would, furthermore, seem undeniable that her scientific interests, particularly palaeobotany, she acquired from her father. But the lessons she learned from her parents were as likely to be negative as positive. The high romantic, almost swooning—a Stopes word—view of love and marriage and the crucial significance of sexual happiness within marriage expressed in *Married Love*, she did not learn at her mother's knee. If anything, they were reactions to a marriage Stopes must have known was increasingly loveless and unhappy. Furthermore, her father bequeathed her financial burdens. His love for palaeontology had led him to neglect his business and his death at the age of 50 left Stopes partly to support both her mother and her increasingly ill sister, Winnie: a situation which did not encourage family harmony. In the end, of course, her own marriages did not meet the standards of *Married Love*: she was eventually to treat her husbands, particularly her second, with even more indifference than her mother did her father. But it would be rash for us to blame her mother for that.

Stopes's early education, however, certainly has the mark of her mother's influence. At her mother's insistence she was educated at home until she was 12, when she went to St George's Girls' High School in Edinburgh, an institution founded by Scottish suffragists.

[8] It would, however, be wrong to assume that Henry was blameless in this. He appears rarely to have sacrificed his own interests for the marriage and always preserved a distance from his wife. As Rose points out, for example, 'it would be difficult to deduce [from his account of their honeymoon] that he was a newly married husband with a pregnant wife' (Rose, *Marie Stopes*, 4).

[9] See her comments on her youthful education: 'Personally I think none but *stupid* children should ever be sent to school till they are at least twelve years old, and I devoutly thank God that I was not' (M. C. Stopes, *Sex and the Young* (London, 1926), 107).

There she was thought to be backward—though backwardness was probably due to the deficiencies of the education her mother had prescribed for her. Two years later, in 1894, she was sent to the North London Collegiate School, in the last term as headmistress of the famous Miss Buss who had founded it. There she flourished—partly because the school took science seriously, especially under Miss Buss's successor, Sophie Bryant. It was clear that Marie was a very able scientist indeed. At the age of 19 she went to University College London and in 1902—after only two years—graduated with first-class honours in botany and third-class honours in geology. Her father lived long enough to hear of her success. She was awarded a University College scholarship which enabled her to go to Munich, where she obtained her doctorate of philosophy (a degree she could not get in England) with a thesis on cycades (a sago-producing branch of the palm family). Her time at Munich was significant not just to her career as a scientist. It was in Munich that the personality and style we associate with her becomes first apparent. This is the Stopes who loved dancing and greatly admired Isadora Duncan (whose ebullience and life force she certainly shared); also the Stopes of elaborate hats and jewellery, flowing and highly coloured silks, and—her mother's daughter—no corsets.[10] Marie's taste, an admirer, Harold Begbie, later wrote, 'is on the bright side of things, and faring forth to a London garden-party, and arrayed in a frock of several joyous colours, she makes rather an unusual picture in the streets'.[11] It was also in Munich that she met the first man with whom she was really in love: Kenjiro Fujii, a 37-year-old Japanese botantist, technically married, and with a child in Japan.

In 1904 Stopes was appointed demonstrator in botany at the University of Manchester and the following year was awarded a D.Sc.,

[10] She was, however, not unaware of the erotic possibilities of corsetry. In *Love-Letters of a Japanese* (see below), Mertyl Meredith [Stopes] wrote to Kenrio Watanabe [Fujii]: 'Sweet, I long so for the physical touch of your hands on mine, and to look into your eyes. To be kissed, I sometimes long so much that I take a girdle and bind it tightly that I can hardly breathe, round my waist and then close my eyes and dream that it is your arms around me. It gives me almost the feeling. You know I have never worn corsets. I have always been scornful of women who did. But you know, dear, this teaches me that this is why so many women like to have them very tight' (G. N. Mortlake (ed.), *Love-Letters of a Japanese* (London, 1911), 104).

[11] H. Begbie, *Marie Stopes: Her Mission and Her Personality* (London, 1927), 13.

the youngest woman in England to obtain one.[12] She and Fujii agreed
to marry. He, however, could not come to Europe. She, therefore,
decided to go to Japan and persuaded the Royal Society to fund a
study of the botanical evolution of angiosperms, flowers which pro-
tect their seeds within a casing (like pods). She arrived in Japan in
August 1907 and remained until January 1909. Although she rather
liked Japan and her work prospered, the relationship with Fujii did
not. The affair was never physically consummated and Stopes
returned to England solo. Characteristically, she recounted her love
for Fujii in the form of an epistolary novel, *Love-Letters of a Japanese* (1911), 'edited' by 'G. N. Mortlake'. Between Fujii and her first
marriage there were two other relationships, both of which foun-
dered: the most serious on Stopes's side was with 'Charlie' Hewitt,
whom she was none too scrupulous in trying to capture.[13] Now successful in her career—she had been appointed lecturer in botany at
Manchester on her return—she still longed for marriage. Such longing led to that crisis in her life from which came *Married Love*. In
1910 she gave up her lectureship at Manchester in order to go to
Canada to study carboniferous flora. At a conference in St Louis in
December 1910 she met a Canadian botanical geneticist, Reginald
Ruggles Gates. He proposed marriage within the week and they were
married less than three months later. Marie returned to England
with Gates.

The marriage, which lasted five years, was a disaster; but quite
why is not entirely clear. Stopes and Gates were certainly different
types: indeed, it is hard to imagine someone less like the reserved,
conventional, deeply religious Gates than she. He also found it difficult to accept her success as a scientist. Gates was himself a distinguished geneticist but in England it was his wife who got the jobs.
As we shall see, he also disliked her feminism and the extent of her
commitment to women's suffrage. Stopes did not help by
introducing into their household Aylmer Maude. Maude was a
biographer of Tolstoy, a practitioner of Tolstoyan politics, and the

[12] Although this introduction is not primarily concerned with Stopes as scientist, it is
important to note how distinguished she was. Her two-volume study of the flora of the
cretaceous age, published by the British Museum, was immediately recognized as a
major work, and the work she did with R. V. Wheeler on the structure of coal remains
standard.

[13] For this episode, see Hall, *Marie Stopes*, 80–6. Hewitt said, perceptively, that Stopes
was 'more in love with Love than with me'.

leading translator of Tolstoy into English. He was also a prominent member of London's literary world. Maude, though married and the father of four sons, was now detached from his wife. Stopes and Maude had met at a dinner-party in 1912 and Maude soon became infatuated with Stopes. She, in a manner of speaking, fell in love with him. She invited him to live with Gates and herself as a lodger, partly because they needed the money. Although Gates had originally agreed to this arrangement, it was a combustible threesome. Not surprisingly, given Stopes's behaviour, he became very jealous of Maude and eventually threw him out; by which time the marriage was dead in the water.[14] The apparent reason for its death, the world was soon to learn, was Gates's impotence and his wife's sexual innocence.

In a famous sentence in the preface to *Married Love* Stopes wrote: 'In my own marriage I paid such a terrible price for sex-ignorance that I feel that knowledge gained at such a cost should be placed at the service of humanity.'[15] In the book and in her play *Vectia* (1926), which the Lord Chamberlain refused to license for production, Stopes claimed an extreme sexual innocence; an innocence way beyond a simple ignorance of the art of love. An innocence which could only be corrected by a sustained course of self-education— mostly in the British Museum. Though this sentence, and all that it implies, has tremendous éclat, we should, however, treat it carefully. It is very unlikely that a scientist, much of whose work was on the reproduction of plants, would be quite so ignorant of human sexuality. Furthermore, we know that in 1911 Stopes had given a desperate clergyman contraceptive advice which appears to have been exactly the same technique she recommended in *Married Love*.[16] In 1916, somewhat surprisingly for her, she gave a girl clear directions on how to induce an abortion ('hot baths and purgatives should be taken. I believe penny royal is used with no danger and satisfactory results'[17]) which again suggests a reasonable acquaintance with human sexuality. Gates made no public comment at the time, but his version of

---

[14] Maude's view of the ménage (which was also Stopes's view) can be found in Aylmer Maude, *Marie Stopes: Her Work and Play* (London, ?1933), 74. Gates 'developed an absurd jealousy and attempted a domination which rendered life intolerable. At that time I was frequently a witness of ridiculous little scenes'.

[15] This sentence appears in every edition of *Married Love*.

[16] For this encounter with the clergyman, see Rose, *Marie Stopes*, 77–8.

[17] Quoted in Hall, *Marie Stopes*, 123. Penny royal was then probably the most common form of purgative and abortifacient.

events was deposited in the British Library after his death. According to him, the marriage was not sexually hopeless but was under-
mined by Stopes's relentless sexuality. She also, he said, constantly
used pessaries. As to her virginity, she had some difficulty in obtaining medical certification of this and the certificate eventually presented to the courts was rather guarded. Whose version is correct we
cannot now know. We do know, however, that presumed sexual dys-
function was the only way Stopes could get out of a failed and
unhappy marriage. As the laws then stood she could obtain a divorce
in neither Canada nor England. Her one recourse was to have the
marriage annulled on the ground of non-consummation; by arguing,
and demonstrating medically, that she was still a virgin after five
years of marriage. This she did and the marriage was dissolved in
1916. Gates did not contest the action. Thereafter, Stopes was necessarily committed to her version. She could have chosen not to have
mentioned it at all in the preface to *Married Love*. But the fact is that
famous sentence gives *Married Love* a kind of dramatic foundation—a sexual narrative: the progress from ignorance to knowledge—which as a rhetorical strategy was almost indispensable to its
success. Nor did she stop at the preface. Her view of the Stopes–
Gates marriage, and of Gates, is perfectly clear from the text of
Married Love itself.[18]

Married Love was born of Stopes's attempts to liberate herself
from Gates; from the constraints of a marriage which fell so far
below her own expectations of what a marriage should be. But these
cannot alone explain the book or Stopes's career thereafter. In many
ways she was a very characteristic figure of the Edwardian period,
and most of the dominant intellectual influences on her were late
Victorian and Edwardian. Although she eventually stood on the
radical wing of the women's suffrage movement her feminism was

---

[18] See p. 91: 'I have known a romantic man of this type ["the self-opinionated male"],
apparently unaware that he was encroaching upon his wife's personality, who yet
endeavoured not only to choose her books and her friends for her, but "prohibited" her
from buying the daily newspaper to which she had been accustomed for years before her
marriage, saying that one newspaper was enough for them both, and blandly ignoring
the fact that he took it with him out of the house before she had an opportunity of
reading it. This man posed to himself more successfully than to others, not only as a
romantic man, but as a model husband; and he reproached his wife for jeopardising their
perfect unity whenever she accepted an invitation in which he was not included.' The
point at issue—her copy of *The Times*—was no doubt genuine, but this is a rather
distasteful paragraph nonetheless.

representative of the Edwardian women's movement. The evidence suggests that she had always believed, even as a student, in more-or-less absolute gender equality in work: that women, at least middle-class women, had a right to use their intelligence in work as well as in motherhood, and that they impoverished themselves and society if they did not do so. She retained her maiden name after her marriage to Gates—though to those of her friends who were enslaved by 'the bonds of custom' she was prepared to be known as Stopes-Gates—and throughout her life she insisted on being called Dr Marie C. Stopes; even when, as during the famous libel suit against Dr Halliday Sutherland, it might have been prudent not to have done so.[19] On 6 April 1914 she wrote to *The Times* protesting against the decision of the London County Council to dismiss medical practitioners who married, and argued that such women would be perfectly entitled to live in unmarried union if that were the only way they could stay in post. 'Three years ago such a course would have filled me with horror.' Stopes was not hostile to men—far from it—but she held the common feminist view that the world was run by men at the expense of women: particularly, on occasion, herself. In 1926, after the banning of her play *Vectia*, she wrote:

What is the women dramatist up against today? Men managers, men producers, men theatre owners, men newspaper proprietors, men critics, men censors, a man-made code of so-called current morality which . . . is a filthy and disgusting farce . . . Our current official standards cover the slavery and torture of women, foster unspeakably degraded displays of sexual vice and racial wickedness. Yet against the current code women's voice is scarcely ever heard, because even if it is raised it is not adequately transmitted through the press or the pulpit because of her economic weakness and dependence.[20]

She was at first more circumspect in her attitude to the women's suffrage movement. Although sympathetic to its aims, she was very

---

[19] For the very revealing exchange between Sutherland's counsel and Stopes see the report of the case in M. Box (ed.), *The Trial of Marie Stopes* (London, 1967), 80. In 1922 Dr Halliday Sutherland, a Catholic convert, accused Stopes of undertaking 'experiments' on poor women via her birth-control clinic in Holloway. Against advice, Stopes sued him for libel. The action, which received enormous publicity, eventually went to the House of Lords where Stopes lost. For details of the case, see R. A. Soloway, *Birth Control and the Population Question in England, 1877–1930* (Chapel Hill, NC, and London, 1982), 247–8.

[20] M. C. Stopes, *A Banned Play and a Preface on the Censorship* (London, 1926), 9.

reluctant to do anything which would obstruct her professional advance, as she freely admitted.[21] She even discouraged her mother from speaking to Manchester students on women's suffrage. By 1912, now well established as a scientist but increasingly unhappy in marriage, she was less circumspect. In that year she joined the Pankhursts' Women's Social and Political Union (the more militant wing of the suffrage movement, a wing she had once thought a 'vulgar byword') and marched with it. She supported women's tax resistance: to the dismay of Gates and Maude, both of whom disliked her involvement in the movement, though for somewhat different reasons.

She was also strongly committed to eugenics—to the belief that human capacities and incapacities, strengths and frailties, are wholly or largely inherited, and to the accompanying belief that some races are genetically superior to others. The politics of eugenics are now so unacceptable that it is easy to forget what a commonplace it was in Edwardian social thought, in the United States and Europe as well as Britain, and as strongly held by scientists as anyone else. Stopes joined the Eugenic Society in 1912, only five years after its foundation, and was briefly a member of the much more dogmatic Malthusian League. Her writing is often markedly eugenic in tone. This was particularly true of the two volumes Stopes conceived as successors to *Married Love*: *Wise Parenthood* (1918) and *Radiant Motherhood* (1920). In *Wise Parenthood*, which is dedicated 'to all those who wish to see our race grow in strength and beauty', she wrote:

From a variety of causes our race is weakened by an appallingly high percentage of unfit weaklings and diseased individuals. The work of the Empire is hindered and its existence jeopardized if our people are so hampered. The majestic destiny of the human race can only be fulfilled when all are strong, beautiful and intelligent. Hence only children with the chance of attaining such a maturity should be conceived.[22]

In later editions, Stopes gave the eugenic theme further emphasis,[23] while in *Radiant Motherhood* the argument was even more polemical:

When [parliamentary] Bills are passed to ensure the sterility of the hopelessly rotten and racially diseased, and to provide for the education of the

---

[21] See Rose, *Marie Stopes*, 42, 53.

[22] M. C. Stopes, *Wise Parenthood* (London, 1918), 7. See also pp. 9–10.

[23] See e.g. *Wise Parenthood* (18th edn. London, 1937), 27–8, 62–4.

child-bearing woman so that she spaces her children healthily, our race will rapidly quell the stream of depraved, hopeless and wretched lives which are at present ever increasing in proportion in our midst.[24]

As her activities became devoted to working-class birth control the tone could lose composure almost completely. In 1919, in an article, 'Mrs Jones Does Her Worst', published in the *Daily Mail* (but rejected by the *Daily Mirror*), she invited the reader to go down any of the 'mean streets' of a British city. 'Are these puny-faced, gaunt, blotchy, ill-balanced, feeble, ungainly, withered children the young of an Imperial Race?' Isn't it, she asked, 'for the leisured, the wise, to go to [Mrs Jones] and tell her what are the facts of life, the meaning of what she is doing and what she ought to do . . . for *Mrs Jones is destroying the race!*'[25] Before the 1922 general election she asked each parliamentary candidate to sign a declaration that if elected he or she would 'press the Ministry of Health to give such scientific information . . . as will curtail the C3 [i.e. the unskilled working class] and increase the A1'. By 1926 she was emphasizing the eugenic dangers of illegitimacy. 'The illegitimate child', she wrote, 'is inherently inferior to the legitimate, through the fact that his mother has failed to maintain her self-respect and the respect of the father', the implication clearly being that such moral qualities as 'respect' are inherited.[26] The moving and depressing collection of letters she received from working-class women, some of which she edited and published as *Mother England* (1929), is pointedly dedicated to 'those who are expected to be the mothers of an imperial race'.

It would be wrong, as Deborah Cohen points out, to suggest that Stopes was an entirely consistent eugenicist. In her clinical practice, Cohen writes, she 'clearly placed the individual woman's happiness over eugenic ideals'.[27] Her personal correspondence with working-class women usually did the same.[28] Nor, as a eugenicist, would she have denied that there were within the skilled working class many who were racially fit. But there was also a tactical element to her

---

[24] M. C. Stopes, *Radiant Motherhood* (London, 1920), 233.

[25] Quoted in Hall, *Marie Stopes*, 173.

[26] Stopes, *Sex and the Young*, 134.

[27] D. Cohen, 'Marie Stopes and the Mothers' Clinics', in Peel (ed.), *Marie Stopes, Eugenics and the English Birth Movement*, 83.

[28] For this, see Lesley A. Hall, 'Marie Stopes and Her Correspondents: Personalising Population Decline in an Era of Demographic Change', ibid. 28.

eugenics: she was careful not to alienate the labour movement, as the trenchantly eugenic Malthusian League had done. Although not always good at politics, she was a very political animal. Furthermore, her feminism, her reputation for 'advanced' views, and her eye for the main chance threw her into the company of the Fabians—especially Bernard Shaw—who held to an increasingly diluted form of eugenics. In her writing, therefore, she made a point of associating the upper working class, the artisan class, with the middle class. In *Radiant Motherhood* she asserted that the 'thriftiest and better of the working class' were battened on by the unfit: 'There is throughout the whole Labour Movement, as throughout the less vocal but deeper feeling of the middle class, a passionate desire to eliminate the misery and human degradation which on every hand to-day saddens the tender conscience.'[29] George Roberts, a former leading Labour MP and minister in the Lloyd George wartime coalition, chaired the famous Queen's Hall meeting (31 May 1921), which Stopes staged to publicize birth control, while J. R. Clynes, then leader of the Parliamentary Labour Party, was conspicuously present.[30] She was also prepared to say publicly— whatever she thought privately—that we are not altogether genetically determined: 'we inherit two-thirds of our nature and make up the rest for ourselves'.[31] Nonetheless, despite her cautious attitude to the artisan class, Stopes never seriously questioned any of the main propositions of the eugenic movement and rarely denied her adherence to them.

Married Love is thus unusual amongst Stopes's writing in not making much of eugenics. Indeed, she specifically makes nothing of eugenic arguments: 'Of the innumerable problems which touch upon the qualities transmitted to the children by their parents, the study of which may be covered by the general term Eugenics, I shall here say nothing.' We can only speculate as to why she did this. She said that many writers had already 'considered these subjects, and my purpose in this book is to present aspects of sex-life which have been more or less neglected by others' (p. 84)—to introduce eugenics would simply clutter the argument. It is also possible she thought, since she was writing for a eugenically superior readership anyway,

---

[29] Stopes, *Radiant Motherhood*, 234–5.
[30] For the meeting, see Briant, *Marie Stopes*, 144.
[31] Quoted in Hall, *Marie Stopes*, 111.

that such discussion was unnecessary. Whatever her thinking, *Married Love* undoubtedly gains from the absence of eugenics.

Stopes was readier than most to use a no-nonsense technical vocabulary (as for example in her descriptions of human sexual physiology) and this owed a good deal to her training as a scientist and something to Havelock Ellis's example. But much of *Married Love*, with this important exception, is written in anything but scientific mode. What struck many contemporaries, and even more strikes the modern reader, is the frequently overcharged, unrestrained style of the book. This is, for example, how Stopes describes the yearning of young men and women for a 'mate':

With the dreams and bodily changes of adolescence, come to the youth and maiden the strange and powerful impulses of the racial instinct. The bodily differences of the two, now accentuated, become mystical, alluring, enchanting in their promise. Their differences unite and hold together the man and the woman so that their bodily union is the solid nucleus of an immense fabric of interwoven strands reaching to the uttermost ends of the earth; some lighter than the filmiest cobweb, or than the softest wave of music, iridescent with the colours, not only of the visible rainbow, but of all the invisible glories of the wave-lengths of the soul. (pp. 17–18)

The description of orgasm was so intense and lyrical that many of Stopes's readers wondered why they had never experienced it or assumed they never could:

The half swooning sense of flux which overtakes the spirit in that eternal moment at the apex of rapture sweeps into its flaming tides the whole essence of the man and woman, and, as it were, the heat of the contact vapourises their consciousness so that it fills the whole of cosmic space. (p. 78)

The book's last, short paragraph is hardly less lyrical:

When knowledge and love together go to the making of each marriage, the joy of *that new unit, the pair* will reach from the physical foundations of its bodies to the heavens where its head is crowned with stars. (p. 106)

Yet there is no particular reason why a scientist should write in a 'scientific' manner, whatever that might be, particularly one who believed that a monogamous marriage was as much a mystical as sexual union. Nor, as we shall see,[32] was she unique in this. Stopes

---

[32] Below, p. xxvii.

was actually writing in a style very recognizable to the Edwardian reader, particularly the reader of late-Victorian and Edwardian novels and poetry. Indeed, we can get a good idea of Stopes's tastes from the epigraphs to the chapters of *Married Love*.[33] Chapter I of *Married Love*, for instance, begins with a long quotation from George Meredith's *Diana of the Crossways* (1885). Meredith was famous for his purple passages, and the quotation, with its mix of the archaic, the high lyric, and the dreamily sensual, might have been written by Stopes herself. In 1912 she wrote down a list of words she thought she should use: they were, *inter alia*, rosemary, sapphire, beryl, amethyst, amber, roseate, ripple, valour, virginal, and vervain—words all too common in the Edwardian romantic novel. Her favourite poets were Edwardian or Georgian—Walter de la Mare, John Masefield, Laurence Binyon, Edmund Blunden, and, strangest of all, Lord Alfred Douglas, once Oscar Wilde's lover and tormenter, whose sonnets she thought the finest in the language and with whom she developed a close, if rather bizarre friendship. Literature meant much to Stopes. She was a member of the Society of Authors and eventually a fellow of the Royal Society of Literature.[34] She wrote huge numbers of novels and poems, and fairy stories for children under the name 'Erica Fay'. Many were never published; though a number of her poems and plays, and one novel (under her own name), were. The older she got, the more she valued literature and the less she valued science.

Stopes was particularly attached to the work of Maurice Hewlett (1861–1923), though his name, unlike Meredith's, does not appear in *Married Love*. Hewlett, to whom Stopes had sent admiring letters even before she wrote *Married Love*, was a very popular author of romantic novels and romances written in a highly mannered style. Some of his books were 'edited' collections of stories, fancies, or letters and often had a quasi-didactic purpose.[35] It was this model— the didactic romance—that Stopes originally intended to follow. She

[33] See Explanatory Notes to pp. 22, 27, 61, 78, and 102 below.

[34] It was as the representative of the Society of Authors on the Cinema Commission of Inquiry set up by the National Council of Public Morals that she met the Bishop of Birmingham, Russell Wakefield, a significantly older man who, like another older man, Aylmer Maude, became strongly attracted to Stopes; and she, in her way, to him.

[35] Maude, *Marie Stopes*, 79–80. Hewlett's *Letters to Sanchia* (1910) is a good example of what Stopes would like to have written. See also *The Forest Lovers* (1898), perhaps his most popular novel, which is a medieval chivalric romance.

openly admitted the influence of Hewlett. 'My original plan', she
wrote, 'had been to convey the help and knowledge in *Married Love*,
not as a strong solution as it now is in one book, but diluted into a
series of novels and romances. The first of these I drafted as a narrative interspersed with poems conveying one of the many facets of the
subject through the medium of a tale.'[36] In 1911 she sent the manuscript of this 'tale' to Hewlett for comment. He replied that 'it is a
kind of first sketch of a thing, which, when complete, might be
romantic, poetical, philosophical . . . but which must be completed
to make it so'.[37] She destroyed the manuscript; only rescuing a couple
of the original poems from the fire. Whether this kind of literature
committed her to a high romantic view of marriage or whether she
read this kind of literature because she always had such a view is
hard to tell. But it probably does not matter much. As Keith Briant,
who knew her well and was her lover for a time in the late 1930s,
wrote: 'All we can say is that she was a woman blessed, or cursed,
from an early age with an impossibly exaggerated idea of the male–
female relationship, which was the reason for the success of her work
and the cause of her own ultimate loneliness.'[38]

One consequence of this 'impossibly exaggerated idea' was her
growing conviction that modern sexology, like realist literature, was
increasingly 'pathological'—as arguably it was; that the needs and
desires of the 'normal' were nowhere met. In the preface to *Married
Love* she wrote:

In the following pages I speak to those—and in spite of all our neurotic
literature and plays they are in the great majority—who are nearly normal, and who are married or are about to be married, and hope, but do not
know how, to make their marriages beautiful and happy. (p. 10)

During the course of her libel action against Halliday Sutherland she
was asked why she had written *Married Love*. 'It is very difficult to
express in a few words,' she answered,

but in a few words it is my belief that the stability of the country, and the
happiness and stability of the home rests on the mutual understanding
and love between a man and a woman who are making that home, in their
marriage, and I know from personal experience and from many con-

---

[36] Quoted in Briant, *Marie Stopes*, 89–91.
[37] Quoted in Hall, *Marie Stopes*, 111.
[38] Briant, *Marie Stopes*, 256.

fidences that owing to the civilisation and other unnatural conditions of our life, the fundamental knowledge which is necessary so that a man and a woman may understand each other, and love each other in the best way, is so often lacking, and it was in order to give the knowledge of the normal right experience and relation between men and women that I wrote this book. I have read, I think, everything written in all the leading languages on the subject of sex relations, and I found that they dealt with abnormalities, some of these leading books with the most horrible abnormalities, but there was nothing that gave guidance to the normally healthy pair who started with love and desired to maintain a loving happy home.[39]

In fact, she had turned against not just a preoccupation with sexual abnormality, but against most of the trends in modern literature. In May 1915 she wrote to Maude:

More and more intensely I do feel that the one thing worth bringing into and trying to increase in the world is love, love and its joy and beauty in every form and every possible expression. That is why I am beginning to revolt against so much of the so-called 'intellectual' works, the gloomy realistic novels, the problem plays—light, trust, joy, the palpitating beauty of simple things and greatly lived. Simply lived lives is what I would like to portray.[40]

Such a view she never abandoned.

Another consequence of her turn against the modern was her belief that urban civilization—city life—was itself destructive of sexual happiness. The overstimulation of the city tended to 'speed-up' men's sexual reactions, while suppressing those of women. Stopes even suggested that since the city provided so few opportunities for 'exploration', men's recourse to prostitutes was one of the few ways they could 'escape into new experiences' (p. 99). The social and literary framework of *Married Love* is, therefore, essentially pastoral:

even for those who have leisure to spend on love-making, the opportunities for peaceful, romantic dalliance are less to-day in a city with its tubes and cinema shows than in woods and gardens where the pulling of rosemary and lavender may be the sweet excuse for the slow and profound mutual rousing of passion. (p. 26)

In one who believed intensely in the romantic idea of the perfect marriage and in the sonnet as the highest form of literature,

---

[39] Box (ed.), *Trial of Marie Stopes*, 77.
[40] Quoted in Hall, *Marie Stopes*, 114.

pastoralism comes as no surprise. But we should remember that a form of pastoral anti-urbanism was characteristic of Edwardian social commentary—in Europe as well as Britain:[41] city life encouraged 'nerviness' and agitation; all the senses were overstimulated; children and adolescents were quick and sharp, but could not concentrate on anything and were easily 'run-down'. The huge Edwardian literature on the 'boy-labour problem' heavily depended on this idea of the city, as did the various back-to-the land movements, plans for garden cities, and the belief that allotments were a necessary therapy for the ills of urban life. In seeing the city as she did, Stopes was in good company.

She was also, more or less *ex hypothesi*, very hostile to deviant sexuality. In *Enduring Passion* (1928) she wrote that 'no woman who values the peace of her home and the love of her husband should yield to the wiles of the Lesbian whatever the temptations to do so'.[42] In *Sex and the Young* (1926) she suggested that precociously developed girls 'should not share a bedroom or bathroom in a boarding school'[43] and argued that the education of children, particularly girls, by unmarried members of their own sex, 'generally accepted as being natural and right' was, on the contrary, 'fundamentally wrong'.[44] There was an element of autobiography in this. While at North London Collegiate School she had a passionate (though almost certainly not physical) relationship with a young teacher, Clothilde von Wyss—a relationship which is alluded to in *Sex and the Young*[45] and which the older Stopes obviously found difficult to accept as part of the business of growing up.

There are several reasons why she should have appeared so hostile to homosexuality. One is that homosexual relationships, however sympathetically interpreted, could never be encompassed by her definition of the ideal marriage. A second is that many eugenicists, including Stopes, thought homosexuality racially dysgenic. While, for instance, a homosexual relationship between two adults was not, she suggested, a 'social crime' (though a 'sin') it was necessarily racially unfruitful. Those men who corrupt boys, however, 'commit

---

[41] See below.
[42] Stopes, *Enduring Passion* (London, 1928), 41.
[43] Stopes, *Sex and the Young*, 26
[44] Ibid. 48–9.
[45] Ibid. 54–5.

a social crime of a revolting nature and may most probably destroy soul and body of these boys rendering them useless as adult husbands and fathers. Hence by this crime the State is deprived of useful citizens for two generations and their potential progeny are destroyed.' Homosexuality in whatever form was, therefore, an attack upon the race.[46] The third reason was sheer prudence. Stopes was very careful to give her enemies no opportunity to prosecute her publications. While she would, therefore, give occasional advice about abortion, she very publicly refused to countenance it as a form of birth control, even in the 1930s when the issue was being seriously considered.[47] She was opposed to premarital sex and the use of contraception before marriage. *Married Love* and its successors were intended for normal, married, monogamous couples—and no one else. As a result, though her play *Vectia* was banned and the film censors obstructed the distribution of a film, *Maisie's Marriage*, in Britain not one of her publications was prosecuted for obscenity. Furthermore, she was always anxious that her causes should be supported by the influential and the famous, and she was aware that the influential and the famous easily take fright. Her sexual revolution was to take place within what was, in many respects, a very conventional sexual morality.

The Origins of Married Love

Thus there was much in Stopes—in her education, cultural and literary inclinations, personality, first marriage, and a certain prudence—that found its way into *Married Love*: equal rights and equal status feminism, the scientist's readiness to use technical and

[46] For Stopes's attitude to homosexuality, see Briant, *Marie Stopes*, 212. For a good example of the eugenic view of homosexuality, see the letter from Sir James Barr (former vice-president of the BMA) to Stopes, 24 Jan. 1922: 'The nation which most effectually adopts eugenic ideals is bound to rule the world. The sexual function should not be repressed in the subconscious mind, we wish to get rid of the Freudian filth which degrades and debases the human species. We may not at once be able to get rid of homosexuals, but an enlightened nation will have no use for them, and they will gradually disappear from the face of the earth which their shadow now darkens' (R. Hall (ed.), *Dear Dr Stopes: Sex in the 1920s* (London, 1978), 97).

[47] She refused to support Rose Witcop and Guy Aldred when they were prosecuted for obscenity after publishing a revised edition of Margaret Sanger's *Family Limitation* (1923), in which there was a veiled reference to abortion (Soloway, *Birth Control and the Population Question*, 230–1).

straightforward language, a lushly romantic view of the relationships between men and women and of the monogamous marriage, and a belief that sexual knowledge made for marital happiness. But *Married Love* did not come from an intellectual vacuum. In her later life, especially during the battles for birth control, Stopes was much criticized for her reluctance, indeed refusal, to acknowledge the work of others—particularly if it anticipated hers. This, however, is not true of *Married Love*. Like the models of 'sexology' she followed, Stopes freely acknowledged the work of others (though she often made it hard to track them down)—even those with whom she disagreed, and in a manual intended for a mass readership, to 'electrify the country' no less, it has a surprisingly complete scholarly apparatus. She made no attempt, for instance, to conceal her indebtedness to F. H. A. Marshall's *The Physiology of Reproduction* (1910) or to the appropriate medical and scientific literature. Nor does she deny the influence of the five people who either shaped much of the argument of *Married Love* or whom she felt, in a sense, she had to confront: Edward Carpenter, Havelock Ellis, Ellen Key, Auguste Forel, and Charlotte Perkins Stetson (better known as Charlotte Perkins Gilman).[48] We should note, however, that apart from the significant exceptions of Edward Carpenter and Havelock Ellis, and despite her mother, in writing *Married Love* Stopes does not appear to have been much influenced by British feminist literature or even to have felt the need to recognize it.

The part Edward Carpenter (1844–1929) played in Stopes's intellectual life is well understood:[49] even though he was, as she must surely have known, both a socialist and a homosexual. He is cited three times in *Married Love*. The first occasion is a direct quotation from *Love's Coming of Age* (1896)—probably Carpenter's most famous book—where he 'beautifully voiced [the] longing' even the most

[48] Keith Briant argued that 'Aylmer Maude is a key figure in Marie Stopes's life and has exercised a very definite formative influence upon her' (Briant, *Marie Stopes*, 84). In a general sense that might be true but there is little evidence—other than in the references to Tolstoy (see below, p. xxxv)—he had much direct influence upon the writing of *Married Love*. In the foreword to *Enduring Passion*, however, Stopes acknowledged that the 'expert reading of my manuscript by Tolstoy's famous biographer, AYLMER MAUDE, was most helpful' (Stopes, *Enduring Passion*, p. xiii). Maude himself says he read the manuscript of *Married Love* and thought it would fail (Maude, *Marie Stopes*, 136).

[49] For the influence of Carpenter and Havelock Ellis, and Stopes's intellectual formation generally, see J. Weeks, *Sex, Politics and Society* (2nd edn., London and New York, 1989), 165, 187–94, 206.

prosaic of us has for a soulmate (p. 19), and twice as epigraphs for chapters (VIII and X). She also took a draft of *Married Love* to Carpenter's cottage in Millthorpe, Derbyshire, for his comments; which were favourable—though in an excess of caution he suggested she might first publish the book in French, then a characteristic strategy for anything conceivably obscene. Ruth Hall has argued that, although many of Stopes's ideas were taken from *Love's Coming of Age*, Carpenter gave her largely a 'framework of mysticism'. Her 'romantic nature responded ecstatically to his vision of true lovers'.[50] There is no doubt truth to this; *Love's Coming of Age* has more than its fair share of ecstatic prose.[51] But there is also much tough sexual politics which found its way into *Married Love*—as well as the odd notion that sperms 'pass through the tissues and affect the general body of the female'; a Stopesian *idée fixe*. A remarkable passage attacks the social and sexual competence of the English upper- and middle-class male—'at present the tool of the Jew and the speculator', only too stupid to know it[52]—which has an echo (as to the incompetence) in Stopes, while his famous description of the position of women in modern society differs little from hers:

The 'lady', the household drudge, and the prostitute, are the three main types of woman resulting in our modern civilisation from the process of the past—and it is hard to know which is the most wretched, which is the most wronged, and which is the most unlike that which in her own heart every true woman would desire to be.[53]

And his account of modern sexuality anticipates the argument of *Married Love*, though expressed more pithily: 'The narrow physical passion of jealousy, the petty sense of private property in another person, social opinion, and legal enactments, have all converged to choke and suffocate wedded love in egoism, lust and meanness.'[54] This is not to suggest that Stopes took the sexual politics of *Married*

[50] Hall, *Marie Stopes*, 90.
[51] See e.g. Carpenter's account of modern sex, which has become prurient and unclean: 'Sexual embraces themselves seldom receive the benison of Dame Nature, in whose presence alone, under the burning sun or the high canopy of the stars and surrounded by the fragrant atmosphere, their meaning can be fully understood: but take place in stuffy dens of dirty upholstery and are associated with all unbeautiful things' (*Love's Coming of Age* (Methuen edn., London, 1914), 16).
[52] Ibid. 28–32.
[53] Ibid. 43.
[54] Ibid. 104.

Love 'from' Carpenter, but it is to suggest that there is more to Carpenter, and so to what Stopes could find in him, than a mere account of love as a mystical union of spirit and flesh, man and woman.

Obvious to any reader of *Married Love* is the influence of Havelock Ellis (1859–1939). Ellis is cited more often than any other author.[55] As he was perhaps the country's leading 'sexologist' this is hardly surprising. Furthermore, as Lesley Hall points out, it is Ellis who first argued that conjugal love was an art which had to be learnt—a proposition central to *Married Love*[56]—and it is unlikely that its centrality did not derive at least partly from Ellis; especially from the chapter 'The Art of Love' in his *Studies in the Psychology of Sex*, vol. vi: *Sex in Relation to Society* (1910). This book is characteristic of its time: an enormous compendium of the literature on sex throughout the ages: exactly the kind of book *Married Love* was not. Although shapeless, however, it was frank, in content, if not always in vocabulary: which is why, amongst other things,[57] there was no English edition until 1937, and why the *Studies* were supposedly confined to a medical readership. Quite apart from its use to Stopes as a source, its frankness was undoubtedly a model.

Even before the publication of *Married Love*, however, Stopes was finding Ellis increasingly distasteful as his own interests (she thought) turned more towards sexual pathology: she said that reading his *Studies in the Psychology of Sex* was like 'breathing a bag of soot'. Their personal relations also deteriorated despite, or perhaps because of, Stopes's continuous attempts to exploit his fame and to recruit him for her causes; and they deteriorated further after Stopes's break with Margaret Sanger. When Sanger complained to Ellis about Stopes's behaviour, he replied that Stopes was 'altogether too ridiculous in her child-like self-glorification not to be easily seen through'.[58] Yet the importance of Ellis to *Married Love* seems undeniable.

---

[55] Eight times.

[56] Lesley A. Hall, *Hidden Anxieties: Male Sexuality, 1900–1950* (London, 1991), 66. See also R. McKibbin, *Classes and Cultures: England, 1918–1951* (Oxford, 1998), 319.

[57] The first volume of the *Studies in the Psychology of Sex*—on homosexuality—was, in a complicated case, successfully prosecuted for obscenity. Thereafter the *Studies* were published in the United States.

[58] For Stopes's relations with Ellis, see P. Grosskurth, *Havelock Ellis: A Biography* (New York, 1985), 373–6. Although in the first English edition of *Sex in Relation to*

An equally obvious presence in *Married Love* is Ellen Key (1849–1926), now scarcely remembered in Britain and virtually absent from the English-language literature on Stopes. Yet before 1914 she was probably the most significant European writer on human social and sexual relationships, a kind of Swedish living treasure, with an international reputation exceeding Carpenter or Ellis. It would have been difficult for Stopes to have written *Married Love* without reference to her, even if only to disagree. Key appears five times in *Married Love*: three times in a neutral sense, as a source; once favourably; once unfavourably (pp. 37, 69, 76–7, 26, and 97) Her conception of love, which had 'so profoundly thrilled the youth of the present day', as the French sociologist Jean Finot rather sourly noted,[59] is close to Stopes's own. For Key, marriage could only succeed when it was synonymous with love. The guiding principle of human morality 'must be the unity of marriage and love'. Once this principle is established: 'it follows that the two lowest expressions of sexual division (dualism) sanctioned by society, namely, coercive marriage and prostitution, will by degrees become impossible, since after the triumph of the idea of unity they will no longer answer to the needs of humanity.'[60] She defined love in terms quite acceptable to Stopes, and in a manner—it is important to note—which we tend to associate with Carpenter or Stopes alone: 'This feeling [love], will gradually win for itself the same freedom in life as it already possesses in poetry. The flowering, as well as the budding of love, will then be a secret between the lovers, and only its fruit will be a matter between them and society. As always poetry has pointed out the way to development.'[61] She and Stopes were also as one on the question of birth control and the race. 'Freedom of love's selection', Key wrote, 'under conditions favourable to the race;

Society Ellis acknowledged Stopes as a pioneer in birth-control practice and literature, his discussion of contemporary marriage guidance literature managed to avoid any mention of *Married Love* (*Studies in the Psychology of Sex*, vi, *Sex in Relation to Society* (London, 1937), 410–11) while he advised the reader that '*Heredity in Man* (1929) by Ruggles Gates is widely regarded as the most thorough general treatise of the subject of eugenics in man to date' (p. 457 n.).

[59] J. Finot, *Problems of the Sexes* (London, 1913), 370. Stopes knew Finot's work and quoted him in *Married Love* (100).

[60] E. Key, *Love and Marriage* (New York and London, 1911), 24.

[61] Ibid. 128–9.

limitation of the freedom, not of love, but of procreation [i.e. contraception], when the conditions are unfavourable to the race—this is the line of life.'[62]

At that point, however, Key and Stopes drew apart. Key argued that women's natural role was the breeding and rearing of children: she did not believe they should or could compete with men 'in the departments of production', and she was deeply critical of the 'fanaticism' of much of the women's movement. Women should abandon parliamentary politics because 'what they can accomplish there with the characteristics peculiar to them, is so insignificant that it does not compensate for the injury which ensues because these characteristics are missing in the home'.[63] In what she called the 'amaternal programme', the fanaticism of the women's movement of the previous generation 'now evinces itself in the error that *equal* rights for the sexes must mean also *equal functions*; . . . that *equality* of the sexes implies *sameness* of the sexes'.[64] Furthermore, she placed her conception of marriage within a broader social system. If marriage were to be synonymous with love, it had to be recognized that some marriages will fail. If love is not present no sexual technique will save a marriage. Key thus argued that people should marry young, but that divorce should be easy and cheap.[65] She was much less attached to monogamous lifelong marriage as such than Stopes.[66] Key was also a socialist—though more in the European sense of the 'social movement'. Marriage and love could only achieve the desired unity within a satisfactory material life. The success of the social movement, therefore, 'broadly speaking—will be the only solution to the marriage question'.[67] While rates of pay remained so low and unemployment so common, 'the blood of men, will continue more and more to be corrupted, and that of women to be impoverished, while waiting for the marriage which might have given to society excellent children born of healthy and happy parents'.[68] As for prostitution, it will continue so long as working women are paid so badly; and the solution to that is trade unions and, if necessary, strikes—not 'prohib-

---

[62] Key, *Love and Marriage*, 150.

[63] E. Key, *The Woman Movement* (New York and London, 1912), 131.

[64] Ibid. 181.

[65] Key, *Love and Marriage*, 311.

[66] See below, pp. l–li.

[67] Key, *Love and Marriage*, 128–9.

[68] Ibid. 139.

itions and tea-meetings'. Key wanted a double redistribution of income: downwards from the upper and middle classes to the working-class, and sideways from men to women. Stopes, though not aggressively anti-socialist, was conservative in her politics, and even at the height of her campaign for working-class birth control never seriously suggested that part of the problem might have been an unjust distribution of income.

In *Married Love* Stopes agreed with Key's conception of love, but disputed her view that women should be confined to a maternal and domestic role, however reshapen:

Ellen Key . . . seems to fear the widening of the married woman's life, and she writes as though the aspiration to do professional and intellectual work of a high order must dwarf and sterilise the mother in the married woman.

She writes of a more northerly people, the Scandinavians, and it may be true of her countrywomen, I do not know. But it is *not* essentially and universally true. I am writing of the English, the English of to-day, and though we also have among us that dwarfed and sterilised type of woman, she forms in our community a dwindling minority. The majority of our best women enter marriage and motherhood, or else long for a marriage more beautiful than the warped mockery of it that is offered them. (p. 97)

She here quoted in support Charlotte Perkins Stetson (1860–1935)—after her second marriage Charlotte Perkins Gilman. Gilman was a very radical feminist. She looked to the wholesale reconstruction of society and of gender relations on the basis of a drastic revision of the division of labour and the professionalization of all work. Her most significant book, *Women and Economics* (1st edn., 1898), was a remarkable statement of a social transformation which went beyond anything contemporaries, or indeed ourselves, were actually likely to achieve, but which expressed a view of gender relations with which Stopes was largely in agreement. In Gilman's view the ideal of marital union was impossible because husband and wife

do not make beds and sweep and cook together, and they do not go down town to the office together. They are economically on entirely different social planes, and these constitute a bar to any higher, truer union than such as we see about us. Marriage is not perfect unless it is between class equals. There is no equality in class between those who do their share in the world's work in the largest, newest, highest ways and those who do theirs in the smallest, oldest, lowest ways.[69]

But women were wholly untrained for the vocation which the sexual division of labour imposed upon them: 'No mother knows more than her mother knew: no mother has ever learned her business; and our children pass under the well-meaning experiments of an endless succession of amateurs.'[70] What must be understood, she argued, was that

it is not woman as a sex who is responsible for this mis-mothered world, but the economic position of woman which makes her what she is. If men were so placed, it would have the same effect. Not the sex-relation, but the economic relation of the sexes, has so tangled the skein of human life.[71]

Stopes, of course, could not agree that the sex-relation was of no significance in the degradation of marriage, but she did agree that the exclusion of women from the largest, newest, and highest forms of work played its part. In doing so she aligned herself with a form of feminism which, though undoubtedly discernible in *Married Love* (see especially pp. 95–8), is often overlooked by its readers.

There is, finally, one other decided presence in *Married Love*: Auguste Forel (1848–1931), the 'famous Professor Forel', as Stopes twice calls him (pp. 19, 29). Forel, a Swiss, was at the time a formidable figure; like Key, someone then very well known to the European educated classes, but, also like Key, representative of a culture now largely disappeared. Forel was not dissimilar to Stopes: he was a distinguished scientist—an entomologist and psychiatrist who regarded science, human sexuality, social relationships, and the 'social question' as all within his expertise. In his memoirs he describes how this happened. It began with the temperance movement, of which he was a leading member. Via abstinence

I was led to the important sexual problem. Here again I saw in all directions the profoundest misery and disaster, due to prejudice, the tyranny of religion, and human stupidity. The perversity of our sexual ethic defied all description. With the campaign against prostitution a beginning should be made of a sexual reform which must lead to a natural and rational sexual selection if our whole civilisation is not slowly to perish.

[69] C. P. Gilman, *Women and Economics* (London and Boston, 1906), 219–20.
[70] Ibid. 293–4.
[71] Ibid. 333.

Three further problems occupied me—that is, the unjust enslavement of the female by the male, devised by man alone in the animal kingdom. I became a zealous apostle of women's right to vote, and of women's rights generally. Secondly, the problem of an international language [Esperanto] . . . And thirdly, the problem of the human races. Which races can be of service in the further evolution of mankind, and which are useless. And if the lowest races are useless, how can they gradually be extinguished?[72]

As this implies, Forel, like Stopes, was a strong eugenicist; but, unlike her, relentlessly and indiscreetly so. Lamenting the relative absence in the world of men and women truly sound 'in mind and body', he argued that we have, on the contrary,

a monstrous superabundance of feeble, sickly, mentally perverted, criminally disposed, idle, treacherous, vain, crafty, covetous, passionate, capricious and untrustworthy individuals, whose claims upon others are inexhaustible, while their own services to society are either valueless or actually harmful.

. . . The greater number of these useless pests owe their faults to an hereditarily defective constitution of the protoplasmic germs which brought them into being; and therefore a sound system of racial ethics demands a rational selection in breeding.[73]

As the last sentence suggests, Forel was utterly committed to birth control on eugenic grounds, as, of course, was Stopes: though in her case not on eugenic grounds alone.[74] Furthermore, Forel, unlike most of Stopes's contemporaries, was interested in sexual practice (if not necessarily the art of love)—how frequently, for instance, a man could legitimately expect sexual intercourse with his wife.[75] Forel's conception of the harmonious marriage was very close to Stopes's; though, like Key, he was more favourable to easy divorce than she. The ideal marriage, he wrote, was 'undoubtedly a monogamous union, resting upon mutual and enduring affection and loyalty, and consummated by the birth of several children'. Such a marriage

[72] A. Forel, *Out of My Life and Work* (London, 1937), 198.

[73] A. Forel, *Sexual Ethics* (London, 1908), 39–40. See the introduction by C. W. Saleeby to the English translation: 'It is the no less than sacred cause of Eugenics or Race Culture that gives the sexual life its meaning and the dignity which it may rightly claim, and it is just because the Swiss thinker sees this and never loses sight of it that his work is so immeasurably raised above the ordinary discussions of marriage, prostitution, venereal disease, and the like' (ibid. 7).

[74] See below, p. xlv.

[75] Stopes cites Forel here. See *Married Love*, pp. 29–30. Less often than he thought, was Forel's answer.

must be completely free, that is to say, both parties must be absolutely equal before the law, and no external compulsion other than that of common obligations towards the children must bind them to one another. To this end a complete separation of property, and a just and proper evaluation of every service performed by the wife as well as the husband are of the first importance.[76]

In a society with civilized social legislation 'the difference which now exists between marriage and free love will be little more than a form'.[77]

Of Forel's work, *Married Love* draws most heavily from the first English edition of *The Sexual Question* (1908). This huge book, not unlike Ellis's *Sex in Relation to Society*, only more so, is a study of sex in its social, physiological, cultural, and historical manifestations. Like *Sex in Relation to Society*, it is the kind of encyclopedia Stopes would not have wished to write. Yet many of its ideas anticipate hers. Forel's definition of love, for instance, is close to Stopes's: probably closer than Ellen Key's. He wrote:

After mature consideration, a man and a woman are led by sexual attraction, combined with harmony of character, to form a union in which they stimulate each other to social work, commencing this work with their mutual education and that of their children . . . The sentiments of love will thus become ever more ideal, and will no longer provide egoism with the soil of idleness and comfort on which it grows like a weed.[78]

He had the same view of town life and its degradations as Stopes:

The individual [in the town] is only known in his own circle. Thus circumstances favour the increase of vice and depravity. In addition to this, the insanitary dwellings, the life of excitement and innumerable pleasures, all tend to produce a restless and unnatural existence. The best conditions of existence for man are contact with nature, air and light, sufficient physical exercise combined with steady work for the brain, which requires exercise as much as the other organs; this is just what is wanting among the poor, in the town and in the factory. Instead of this they are offered unhealthy nocturnal pleasures and a prostitution which spreads itself everywhere with all the dangerous effects we have described.[79]

[76] Forel, *Sexual Ethics*, 44.

[77] A. Forel, *The Sexual Question: A Scientific, Psychological, Hygienic and Sociological Study for the Cultured Classes*, English adaption by C. F. Marshall (London and New York, 1908), 384–5.

[78] Ibid. 114. Italics his.

[79] Ibid. 328.

And, of course, he regarded the 'complete' emancipation of women as indispensable to marital and sexual harmony; to the attainment, indeed, of a sexual Utopia.[80]

We can no more argue of Forel than of anyone else that his ideas were the basis of *Married Love*: much of what he and Stopes argued was in practice the common coin of early twentieth-century 'progressive' sexual sociology. And *Married Love* is both too singular and eclectic a book to be attributed to a source other than its author. But Stopes probably owed more to Forel—an 'exceptionally advanced and broad-minded thinker' (p. 29 n. 1)—than anyone else, Ellis included, even though she was not uncritical of him, and in later editions of *Married Love* was to modify significantly her original approval (p. 34) of his adamant views on prostitution.[81] Where she differed from Forel was in the relatively unsystematic nature of her sexual politics. Forel said of his intellectual and political concerns: 'alcoholism, social problems, psychiatry, penal law, and science are inseparably connected'.[82] If Stopes thought her intellectual and political concerns were inseparably connected, she concealed it well. Nor, unlike Forel or Key, did she believe that marital love could thrive only after a social and economic transformation. In the end, however, this lack of system was much to her advantage. The sheer remorselessness of Forel's eugenicism, for example, is one reason why he is now almost forgotten, whereas Stopes, whose eugenicism was always politically adjustable, is very much remembered. Nonetheless, *Married Love*, for all its singularity and success, did not come from the blue: it is but one example of a large literature, as much Continental and American as British, and could not have been written without it.

Married Love: *Its Publication and Popularity*

The outbreak of the First World War found Stopes inhabiting a tent on the Northumberland coast, there attempting to recover her poise after the disagreeable end of her marriage to Ruggles Gates. She had with her several drafts of what was to become *Married Love*—at this stage (and until the eve of publication) called 'They Twain', a

---

[80] Ibid. 504.
[81] For the modification, see below, pp. xxxix–xli.
[82] Forel, *Out of My Life and Work*, 192.

Stopesian title which, had she persisted in it, would almost certainly have killed the book at birth.[83] She had begun making notes for the book in February 1914 and had also started to measure the pattern and timing of her own sexual desires. The notion of a Hewlett-style romance was definitely abandoned. Stopes later attributed this decision to the First World War. 'Then came the war,' she wrote. 'As it progressed I saw more and more clearly that what the world wanted was not the themes diluted into novels, which might or might not be interesting, but help in some form direct, swift and simple.'[84] *Married Love*, as Jack Coldrick argues in the context of the attitude of the churches to birth control, 'not only represents a landmark in the progress of liberal sexual values and women's rights; it also represents an important document of the First World War and can only be understood in that context'.[85] In *Married Love* itself Stopes emphasized its 'simplicity': 'The whole is written simply, and for the ordinary untrained reader' (p. 10). That the war was crucial in the book's development we must, however, take on trust. What, after all, immediately strikes the reader is the absence in the book of any reference whatever to the disaster overtaking the European middle classes and the culture from which *Married Love* emerged. Furthermore, the decision to abandon the book as a series of romances had been taken well before the outbreak of war. And while 'They Twain'/*Married Love* went through several drafts during the war, there is little evidence that the war much determined the final outcome.

We do know that the various drafts were widely circulated and discussed—in part, of course, as an attempt to secure publication. In October 1914 a draft was sent to E. H. Starling, professor of physiology at University College London, who replied helpfully and later agreed to write a prefatory letter to the published book: an important catch since Starling had an international reputation for his work on the action of chemicals in the blood—indeed, the word hormone is

---

[83] She quoted the words from which this title came in the last chapter of *Married Love*: 'they twain shall be one flesh' (p. 103). The quotation, though arch, is pertinent to the subject, and comes from Matthew 19: 5–6: 'And said, For this cause [marriage] shall a man leave father and mother, and shall cleave to his wife: and they twain shall be one flesh? Wherefore they are no more twain, but one flesh. What therefore God have joined together, let not man put asunder'.

[84] Quoted in Briant, *Marie Stopes*, 91.

[85] J. Coldrick, *Dr Marie Stopes and Press Censorship of Birth-Control* (Belfast, 1992), 4.

his. She also sent it to her co-author on coal, R. V. Wheeler, and the biologist Peter Chalmers-Mitchell, who were much less sympathetic. Others also shied away. Her friend and admirer Bishop Wakefield declined to write a preface, as did Dean Inge, the famous 'gloomy dean' of London who as a eugenicist was sympathetic to Stopes. For both, of course, it was too risky. In July 1915 Stopes discussed the text with Margaret Sanger, and though Sanger exaggerated her influence on Stopes, the celebrated Chapter IX, the 'birth-control' chapter, was probably a result of this meeting. As we have seen, Stopes went through a draft with Edward Carpenter and copies were sent to leading members of the Malthusian Society, including its secretary, Binnie Dunlop. Aylmer Maude read the text; the references to Tolstoy certainly came from him.[86]

Finding a publisher proved more difficult than perfecting the text. Blackie's, who had published her first two books, declined *Married Love*—partly on the ground that the war was the worst, rather than the best moment to publish it.[87] Unwin also refused it, to Sir Stanley Unwin's later regret.[88] Stopes even hoped, in her determination, that the National Council of Public Morals might be persuaded to publish it. In the end, the small firm of A. C. Fifield showed an interest, but demanded a subsidy. Binnie Dunlop had told Stopes that, were she to have problems with publication, he could probably find her 'a rich young man' to help. The rich young man was Humphrey Verdon Roe (1878–1949), a eugenicist who wished to promote working-class birth control and who had (unsuccessfully) offered St Mary's Hospital, Manchester funding to establish a birth-control clinic. Roe was 39 when he met Stopes and was serving in the Royal Flying Corps. He and his brother, Alliott Verdon Roe, had founded the

---

[86] The references are to Tolstoy's asceticism (pp. 74–5) and his views on sexual intercourse during pregnancy (p. 83).

[87] Walter Blackie wrote to her on 13 July 1915 that 'there will be few enough men for the girls to marry and a book would frighten off the few' (Rose, *Marie Stopes*, 88).

[88] Unwin's refusal is a curious story. At the same time as Stopes offered him *Married Love* he was offered 'a novel by an attractive girl . . . dealing with homosexuality and conscientious objection'. Unwin wanted to take *Married Love* on the grounds that it would sell but to refuse the novel on the grounds that it would be prosecuted. His colleague, C. A. Reynolds, wanted the novel and not *Married Love*. Since neither man would budge both books were declined. The novel was, however, published by C. W. Daniel, who was indeed prosecuted, and fined. Unwin, who had suggested Daniel to the novelist, felt obliged to pay part of the fine (S. Unwin, *The Truth about a Publisher* (London, 1960), 137–8).

great aircraft manufacturing firm of Avro and, although Humphrey withdrew from Avro in 1917, he remained a very wealthy man. Dunlop introduced Stopes to Roe in February 1918 and Roe sent her a cheque for £100 to subsidize publication. It was repaid within the month. A few months later Stopes and Roe were married, on 16 May 1918 in a registry office, and on 19 June—at Stopes's insistence—in church. The service was conducted by the Bishop of Birmingham and the bride was given away by Aylmer Maude: something both must have done with very mixed feelings. Although she was later to treat Roe wretchedly, there seems little doubt that the marriage, for a few years at least, gave both happiness. It also gave Stopes the children she craved: Henry, to her bitter grief stillborn, in July 1919, and Harry, a very healthy boy, in March 1924.

Married Love sold 2,000 copies in its first fortnight of publication and within a year six editions had been published. Stopes had indeed electrified the country. But who was electrified? For whom did she write this remarkable book? Although she made little of it, Stopes was in fact quite explicit. In an explanatory footnote in *Married Love* she wrote:

In this, and in most of the generalisations found in this book, I am speaking of things as they are in Great Britain. While, to a considerable extent, the same is true of America and the Scandinavian countries, it must be remembered all through that I am speaking of the British, and primarily of our educated classes. (p. 22)

And this remained true of all of what we might call her 'marriage-guidance books'. In *Radiant Motherhood*, for example, in another footnote explaining for whom that book was written, she repeated exactly the words quoted above.[89] Furthermore, all the material assumptions that underlie these books are upper middle class. In *Married Love*, Stopes advised husband and wife to have separate bedrooms—though she recognized the finances might not always allow it—so that men should escape 'most of the unlovely and even ridiculous proceedings of the toilet'. A husband, however, should be permitted to see 'a beautiful woman floating in the deep, clear water of her bath' (p. 71). When urging total trust as an essential component of married love, she argued that husband and wife 'should each be free to go unchallenged by a thought on solitary excursions, or on

[89] Stopes, *Radiant Motherhood*, 38 n.

visits, weekends or walking tours' (p. 94). In *Radiant Motherhood*, she advised the expectant mother 'to take warm comfortable sitz baths [hip baths] every evening, and she should lie down for at least half-an-hour or an hour in the middle of the day or early evening'.[90] In *Enduring Passion*, she suggested that the best way a run-down woman could recover her vitality was 'to combine a rich, wholesome diet, a good iron tonic, and a visit to a bracing, sunshiny, vitalising locality such as the Swiss Mountains in winter'.[91] This is a whole world away from the grim, deprived proletarian territory of *A Letter to Working Women* (1919) or *Mother England* (1929). Indeed, it is doubtful whether Stopes ever thought successful married love—as she understood it—was possible outside the 'educated classes'. It is also evident from the huge correspondence which Stopes invited and received that the readership of *Married Love* was very largely from the educated classes.[92] Her comment, that *Married Love*, was, amongst other things, based upon 'confidences from men and women of all classes and types' (p. 9), while not necessarily untrue, gives a misleading impression of the book. We should note one further fact here: *Married Love* is dedicated 'to young husbands and all those who are betrothed in love'—a dedication as pointed as the dedication in *Mother England*.

Stopes called *Married Love* 'this little book' and so it is. It contains eleven short chapters, but a rather elaborate prolegomenon. While it went through many editions and revisions, the first edition (March 1918) and the seventh (May 1919) are the two which really matter[93]—though there is an important insertion in the eighth edition (May 1920). Of these editions, the first is obviously the more important. The Oxford World's Classics edition is based on the first edition and the reader thus needs no précis of it here. But the seventh edition introduced some significant changes; not by subtraction, but by addition and emphasis. It would seem useful, therefore,

[90] Stopes, *Radiant Motherhood*, 90–1. After reading *Radiant Motherhood* Mary Stocks concluded that the average family would need at least one thousand pounds a year to purchase the desired radiance.

[91] Stopes, *Enduring Passion*, 68.

[92] For this correspondence, see below, p. xlvi.

[93] For full details of the publishing history of *Married Love*, see P. Eaton and M. Warwick, *Marie Stopes, A Checklist of her Writings* (London, 1977), 23–6.

to give the reader some idea of what these changes were and why Stopes decided to make them.

The first significant change was to the prolegomenon. Stopes, in her understandable anxiety to make the book as acceptable to educated opinion as possible, had induced a medic, Jessie Murray, a personal friend, to write a preface and E. H. Starling and Father Stanislaus St John SJ to write prefatory letters. Stopes herself wrote the author's preface—that which lamented her own sexual ignorance[94]—and an aggressive response to Father St John's letter. His letter, as the reader will see, praised the marriage-guidance aspect of the book but inevitably took exception to its advocacy of birth control. His defence of the Church's position does not read well today and did not read well to Stopes—though he could hardly have been expected to say anything else; hence her spirited reply. She did not, however, tell him that she intended to reply. He was understandably dismayed by this and repeatedly asked her to remove his letter. This she did not do until the seventh edition. But Stopes was always reluctant to end a quarrel with the Catholic Church, and her preface to the seventh edition was in effect a rewriting of her reply to Father St John of the previous six editions. The last paragraph of the preface to the seventh edition is taken verbatim from that reply.[95] The reply to Father St John has one further implication. It strongly suggests that birth control in itself was already becoming uppermost in Stopes's mind; something confirmed by the publication of *Wise Parenthood* at the end of 1918.

Chapter I, 'The Heart's Desire', is unchanged and there is no reason, given its function as a rather romantic introduction, why she should have changed it. In Chapter II, 'The Broken Joy', there is one important addition. To the paragraph (p. 24) which writes of 'the corrosive horror of all aspects of prostitution' she has added a further sentence on 'the horrors unimaginable' of venereal disease.[96]

---

[94] See above, p. xii.

[95] With one exception. The sentence in the first edition which reads: 'Now it seems to me that religious people—and even in your letter I fancy that I detect the same tendency (forgive me if I am wrong)—are too ready to separate this world and the next, to act unreasonably or cruelly here and to trust to Eternity, or the Hereafter, to put all right' (p. 14), reads in the seventh: 'It seems to me that orthodox religious people are too ready to separate this world and the next, to act unreasonably and to trust to Eternity, or the Hereafter, to put all right' (pp. 20–1).

[96] Stopes, *Married Love* (7th edn., London, 1919), 36.

Although she had the standard feminist/eugenic view of venereal disease—that it destroyed the family and the race—there were, as we shall see, 'political' reasons why she should have added this sentence.[97] Stopes made two changes to Chapter III, 'Woman's "Contrariness"'; one slight, one more important. The first simply provides another example of the sexual ignorance of well-brought-up girls to that already provided on p. 33.[98] The second is undoubtedly more significant since it involves prostitution, and additions relating to prostitution, not just in Chapter III but Chapter X also.

Even in the first edition there is a certain ambivalence in Stopes's attitude to prostitution. While holding to the standard condemnations, she notes, as we have seen, that one of the few ways men can 'explore' new experiences in the modern city is via prostitution.[99] In Chapters III and X this ambivalence is, so to speak, explicit. In Chapter III she writes:

Many men who enter marriage sincerely and tenderly may yet have some experience of bought 'love.' It is not then unlikely that they may fall into the error of explaining their wife's experience in terms of the reaction of the prostitute. They argue that, because the prostitute showed physical excitement and pleasure in union, if the bride or wife does not do so, she is 'cold' or 'under-sexed.' They may not realise that often all the bodily movements which the prostitute makes are studied and simulated because her client enjoys his climax best when the woman in his arms simultaneously thrills.

As Forel says . . . 'The company of prostitutes often renders men incapable of understanding feminine psychology, for prostitutes are hardly more than automata trained for the use of male sensuality. When men look among these for the sexual psychology of women they find only their own mirror.' (p. 34)

But the quotation from Forel does not support what Stopes is wishing to argue. In the seventh edition, immediately after the quotation from Forel, she inserted the following paragraph, which renders Forel even more a non sequitur.

Yet the simulated transports of the prostitute have their meretricious value only because they imitate something real, something which should

---

[97] See below, p. xli.
[98] The 'highly educated lady intimately known to me'.
[99] See above, p. xxi.

sweep over every wife each time she and her husband unite. The key which unlocks this electric force in his wife must reverently be sought by every husband, and its place varies in different women.[100]

Something similar happens in Chapter X. In the first edition she writes:

Women feel a so righteous and instinctive horror of prostitution, and regarding it they experience an indignation so intense, that they do not seek to understand the man's attitude.

   The prostitute, however, sometimes supplies an element which is not purely physical, and which is often lacking in the wife's relation with her husband, an element of charm and mutual gaiety in pleasure.

   If good women realised this, while they would judge and endeavour to eliminate prostitution no less strenuously, they might be in a better position to begin their efforts to free men from the hold that social disease has upon them. (p. 99)

These three paragraphs do not themselves represent a very serious criticism of prostitution. On the contrary, they are rather a criticism of the limitations of 'civilized' sexual technique. In the eighth edition she further emphasized these limitations by adding the following two sentences to the second paragraph immediately above:

The prostitute also generally knows many of the subtleties and peculiarities of the stimuli which give not only an added physical delight but an increased completeness and therefore an enhanced health value to the normal act of union. A wife should not be content (as too many wives are) to be a meek and passive instrument for her husband's 'indulgence', she has an active part to play. Without mutual participation neither can fully complete the joint consummation.[101]

The prostitute was thus a professional in the art of sex: she gave for money what a wife should give for love. In effect, Stopes was arguing that one of the stock criticisms of the prostitute—that she merely simulated sexual pleasure and energy—was immaterial. Why she did what she did was of less importance than the fact that she did it, and that men took pleasure in what she did. The increasing tendency for Stopes to see in the prostitute a model for sexual technique, in fact, follows naturally from her belief that an inventive and open sexuality was essential for marital fulfilment. Yet for someone who was

---

[100] Stopes, *Married Love* (7th edn.), 54.
[101] Stopes, *Married Love* (8th edn.), 176.

anxious to remain within the bounds of convention this was a belief to be expounded with care. That the prostitute represented an ideal of married sexuality was, on the whole, not something acceptable to conventional opinion. Thus Stopes's argument is more underhand than it might have been; and is further protected by the addition of the sentence on the 'horrors unimaginable' of venereal disease already noted.[102]

In the seventh edition there is some textual readjustment to Chapter IV, 'The Fundamental Pulse'—which propounds Stopes's Law of the Periodicity of Recurrence in women's sexual desires ('the underlying waves of her primitive sex-tides', p. 39), the notion that women are more sexually alive at certain moments, and that these moments are largely physiologically determined—but no change to the overall argument.

Chapter V, 'Mutual Adjustment', is the first chapter to which Stopes made substantial changes. In the general architecture of *Married Love* this is an important chapter. It actually describes in physiological detail what happens during sexual intercourse and is also a kind of manual of sexual technique. Together with Chapter IX it is what made the book sensational. In the seventh edition Stopes extends her discussion of the marriage night; now lamenting the ignorance of so many men as well as the ignorance of virgin women she lamented in the first edition. A measure of her increasing confidence, her readiness to ignore taboos, are the additions she made to her discussion of sexual technique. They include two new paragraphs which became celebrated:

A rigidity of mental as well as physical capacity seems to characterise some excellent and well-meaning people, and among those whose marriages fail to reach the height of perfection in a physical sense which they

---

[102] In this sense—that Stopes had to be extremely cautious in her treatment of prostitution—Ettie Rout's criticisms are not altogether fair. Rout, a New Zealander who admired Stopes but specialized in telling her home truths, wrote to her that all 'parts of the British Empire have become broader in sex matters in the last ten years—particularly in the last five years. Rationalism and socialism are partly responsible and Continental literature (Ellen Keys [*sic*] etc) and of course Havelock Ellis and Wells and Shaw and Carpenter and many others . . . Briefly, I think you take far too high a view of modern marriage and far too low a view of prostitution. I've know prostitutes who were much finer than some members of the Married Women's Trade Union and many cases where monogamy was the extreme penalty of the law' (Rout to Stopes, 21 Feb. 1921, in R. Hall (ed.), *Dear Dr Stopes*, 93). Stopes, of course, would not necessarily have disagreed with this.

intellectually desire are those who are entirely ignorant that sex-union may be accompanied in many various positions, or those who consider any other position but the most usual one to be wrong.

Yet, curiously enough, it sometimes comes to light that a pair do not even know the usual position, and in my own experience, several couples who have failed to have children, or have failed to obtain the complete delight of union, have revealed that the woman did not know that it is not only her arms which should embrace her lover. Consequently, entry was to him both difficult and sometimes impossible.[103]

An important element of this chapter is Stopes's discussion of premature or excessively speedy ejaculation. She argued that one of the main reasons Anglo-American women were sexually unfulfilled was that their husbands achieved orgasm too soon—a result of sexual ignorance and a disregard for the sexual needs of their wives. In the seventh edition this argument was elaborated. Men, she now wrote, must not only learn to woo their wives, but to master their own impulses: 'the hastiness of most healthy men is largely due to mental ignorance alone, and can be conquered by a persistent and consciously exerted will.'[104]

The chapter most effected by changes in the seventh edition is Chapter IX, 'Children'. Here there are lengthy additions to Stopes's original discussion of sex during pregnancy and of infertility. In the first edition she argued that women should not have intercourse during the last six months of pregnancy—though she conceded many women still wanted it (pp. 82–3). In the seventh edition she was less willing to make a firm judgement, and concluded that

it seems probable that any desire for moderate and careful sex-union between the prospective mother and the father of the coming child should be gratified in the interests of all three. But this opinion is expressed merely provisionally, and largely in response to a number of inquirers who have asked me about this point. Immoderate and excessive desire for sex-union must undoubtedly be looked upon as an unfavourable symptom, and a practising doctor should be consulted about it.[105]

---

[103] Stopes, *Married Love* (7th edn.), 90–1.

[104] Ibid. 94.

[105] Ibid. 137. There was also some dotty psychology in the seventh edition. 'From one distinguished medical specialist,' Stopes wrote, 'I have acquired the interesting suggestion that in one or two cases among his own patients, where the prospective mother had desired unions and the husband had denied them thinking it in her interest, the doctor had observed that the children seemed to grow up restless, uncontrollable, and with an unduly marked tendency to self-abuse.' Stopes thought this a 'most important and suggestive idea' (pp. 136–7).

She also suggested various 'safe' forms of intercourse during pregnancy.

In the first edition there are only three paragraphs about infertility—though they include an adventurous discussion of artificial insemination by donor (pp. 84–5). In the seventh there are four pages. Much of this further material is medical-physiological—ways in which infertility can be overcome, either medically or by changes in sexual technique; some of it is a rather familiar neo-Edwardian socio-psychology:

A woman in modern society who is in a highly nervous condition, which may find expression in her constant need of cigarettes or excitement, may be (though this is by no means universally true) frequently impregnated and at the same time continually throwing off the impregnated ovum before the settling down of that ovum, which results in true conception, can take place. If, therefore, the woman finds herself continuously smoking, or notes in herself any other indication of a lack of placidity in her nerves, she would do well—not merely to restrict her smoking, which is nothing but a symptom of a deeper need—but she would do well to restore as far as possible a calm poise to her whole system by longer sleep, more country air, plenty of fresh butter, or whatever simple remedy it may be that will supply her nerves with something lacking, and for which she is unconsciously craving.[106]

There is a much shorter addition in this chapter to her discussion of birth control. Given Stopes's later fame as a birth controller it is surprising that in a chapter substantially devoted to the case for family planning, there is little—indeed virtually nothing—on the mechanics of birth control.[107] In 1933 Stopes said that was so because she thought little was necessary: 'the control of conception [being] a *sine qua non* in all intelligent married life'.[108] In the seventh edition of *Married Love*, however, she inserted a brisk sentence: 'As a deplorable ignorance on this subject has resulted in many deleterious methods being irresponsibly advocated and widely used, I have felt it necessary to discuss the medical details of the wholesome methods in a little volume apart, "Wise Parenthood".'[109]

---

[106] Stopes, *Married Love* (7th edn.), 147–8.

[107] She refers rather vaguely to the use of spermicides—quinine or vinegar and water or 'other substances'—as a form of contraception.

[108] M. Stopes, *Roman Catholic Methods of Birth Control* (London, 1933), 98.

[109] Stopes, *Married Love* (7th edn.), 156–7. In later editions she added a second sentence: 'In this [*Wise Parenthood*] the ethical and physiological aspects of various methods

The overall effect of these changes to the seventh and eighth editions was to emphasize sexual technique and knowledge—the art of love—and, via *Wise Parenthood*, contraception. They also made the book somewhat more explicit. But they did not significantly modify the argument, which in the three editions remained essentially the same. Broadly speaking it was based upon six propositions.

1. The state of the modern middle-class marriage was, for most married couples, desperate; and the reason for this desperation was sexual unhappiness. Marriage, begun in hope, ended in despair as men and women found their sexual lives increasingly unrewarding. Those who admitted that their sexual lives were unhappy but still insisted that their marriages were a success—as some of Stopes's correspondents did—were deceiving themselves. The 'contrary', disappointed woman and the cross, frustrated man were a product of the modern marriage.

2. Easier and freer divorce, Stopes believed, was no answer, even though a number of her contemporaries argued that it was. While sexual ignorance remained the norm, the acquisition of a new spouse, far from being an answer to the problem, merely multiplied the misery.

3. Only knowledge could dispel misery because it alone dispelled ignorance. Knowledge could restore our healthy instincts, which had been suppressed by the 'artificiality' and 'neurosis' of Anglo-American civilization. There were two kinds of knowledge. An old-fashioned (though rarely known) physiological one: what actually happens during intercourse; and a new one, of which Stopes was in her own mind a discoverer. The new knowledge was based upon an understanding of the sexual 'timetable' of women—the Law of the Periodicity of Recurrence of Women's Desire—and a new art of love which emerged from this understanding. The art of love would re-establish the natural and legitimate role of sexual intercourse as one of the most profound and ecstatic of human experiences.

4. To achieve this men had to change their ways. This was the point of the book's dedication and one of its most important arguments. Men must learn to woo their wives; to recognize, as the moral conventions and gender hierarchies of modern society do not, that

are also considered, and that which is, from all points of view, physiologically best is advocated.'

women's sexual desires are as strong and as legitimate as their own, though more 'seasonal'. They must learn their wives' 'seasons', the moments when women are most sexually alive and desiring, learn to heighten their own sexual pleasure by an informed control rather than a depressing abstinence. Each act of intercourse ('union') should be something new and unexpected. The mystery of sex should be preserved; if possible by the physical circumstances of middle-class life: separate bedrooms or separate holidays, for example.

5. Marriage should be crowned by children. But marital happiness could only be preserved if children were actually wanted and could be raised as they deserve to be raised, and if childbirth did not endanger the health of the mother. A planned family, and thus birth control, was the sine qua non—as Stopes said—of married love.

6. While the problems of the modern marriage were primarily sexual, those problems were in themselves a manifestation of the social exclusion of women. A marriage could only be truly happy when it was between genuinely equal partners, when women were as much participants in the life of the intellect and of the world as men. The 'best women' now sought not just marriage and motherhood but cultural and social creativity, and married love would never be complete until they had it.

The book was an immediate sensation, and its sales huge from the moment of publication. Why was this? Undoubtedly, the main reason was notoriety. By contemporary standards, this was a very explicit book in its description of sexual intercourse and human sexual physiology. Notoriety sells books; especially sexual notoriety. It was the more notorious in that the book was designed for a mass readership. Much existing sexual literature adhered all too closely to the canons of German scholarship, whereas Stopes got down to the problem of marital sexuality 'without climbing the evolutionary ladder and covering the globe first'.[110] Notoriety was accelerated by the attempts to ban the book in the United States and the mobilization

[110] R. Porter and L. Hall, *The Facts of Life: The Creation of Sexual Knowledge in Britain, 1650–1950* (New Haven and London, 1995), 209. In 1919 Stopes told a correspondent: 'if you can find another book on sex in which there is so little about savages and the lower animals, I will give you 6d.'

of an immensely distinguished cohort of writers in its support.[111] Furthermore, the reviews of the book were favourable, if sometimes reserved: it was even reviewed favourably in the *Lancet* and the *British Medical Journal*—the latter praising 'its more than common courage'. Neither, however, mentioned birth control; a revealing omission—unlike the reviewer in the *Times Literary Supplement* who noted cautiously (but did note) that Stopes 'is on the side of those who do not give an unqualified opposition to the control of birth'.[112]

Notoriety alone, however, cannot explain *Married Love*'s success. It was clearly a book whose moment had come. Obvious from the volume of correspondence Stopes received on the book's publication was the extent of sexual ignorance and unhappiness in the country; the feeling shared by so many that *Married Love* and Stopes were their only recourse. In the first edition she had invited women readers to provide her with evidence as to their sexual 'rhythms' in order to lend support to her 'Law'. What she received was an avalanche of correspondence—from almost as many men as women— little of which had to do with her Law but everything to do with sexual unhappiness.[113] This enormous correspondence constitutes a history of the British middle class as much as *Mother England* constitutes a history of the working class.[114] The historian soon discovers that many families have a Marie Stopes story: of the brown-paper covered book everyone concealed but surreptitiously consulted. Nor is all the evidence folkloric. Naomi Mitchison, the writer, found parts of the book a revelation, even though she was married and a mother when she read it. She sent a second copy to her husband in

---

[111] The cohort included Arnold Bennett, Havelock Ellis, George Bernard Shaw, H. G. Wells, May Sinclair, E. Phillips Oppenheim, and A. E. W. Mason.

[112] *Times Literary Supplement*, 11 Apr. 1918. For a summary of the reviews, see Begbie, *Marie Stopes*, 23–4; L. Hall, *Hidden Anxieties*, 8; J. Peel, 'Contraception and the Medical Profession', *Population Studies*, 18/2 (Nov. 1964), 11.

[113] For analyses of this correspondence, see R. Hall, *Dear Dr Stopes*, 215–18; Rose, *Marie Stopes*, 116; Ellen M. Holtzmann, 'The Pursuit of Married Love: Women's Attitude toward Sexuality and Marriage in Great Britain, 1918–1939', *Journal of Social History*, 16/2 (Winter, 1982), 48.

[114] There appears to have been only a small working-class readership for Stopes's books. Working-class correspondence tended to follow her articles in newspapers and magazines, and the volume of the correspondence suggests that these articles were widely read. Yet we do not know how widely. None, for instance, of Elizabeth Roberts's respondents mentioned Stopes when asked how they acquired sexual knowledge (E. Roberts, *A Woman's Place: An Oral History of Working-Class Women, 1890–1940* (Oxford, Blackwells, 1984), 95).

Italy, instructing him to read it before they met again.[115] Historians have noted how far correspondents tended to adopt Stopes's language, which suggests people had no way themselves of articulating their sexual attitudes.[116] To the degree that norms for successful sex were established, it is likely that Stopes—so empty was the field— established them. Mary Stocks argued that what many thought a defect of the book—its stylistic excesses—actually contributed to this. *Married Love* 'was written with a force of religious passion and flamboyant phraseology which enabled it to penetrate the consciousness of millions of inarticulate, ill-instructed married couples, in innumerable obscure homes. Seldom, if ever, has a book brought more happiness to more people.'[117] Nor should we forget that *Married Love* was a little book. Stopes quite deliberately kept it brief: it had none of the historical and anthropological disquisitions of Ellis or Forel. We cannot imagine giving *Sex in Relation to Society* or *The Sexual Question* to a bridal couple on the eve of their wedding; but we can imagine giving them *Married Love*.

Neither should we overlook the significance of a book which emphasized sex as pleasure—even, or perhaps especially, sex 'constrained' by the institution of marriage. However else the First World War might or might not have influenced the writing of *Married Love*, it certainly accelerated something noticeable in the years immediately before 1914: a willingness in many quarters to disentangle marital sexuality from reproduction and to accept sexual pleasure within marriage as itself legitimate. It was on the basis of such legitimacy that Stopes played her trump. Thus, despite the ambivalence towards sexual pleasure common in British society at the time,[118] there is every reason to think that a book which argued that sex *should* be pleasurable, indeed joyous, was one people were very happy to read. At any rate, it was a view of sex nearly all later marriage-guidance manuals felt obliged to adopt.[119] Moreover, Stopes gave an active sexual role to women; *Married Love* legitimated women's sexuality and sexual desires. That ran up against a strong feminist tradition which emphasized the constraining of male sexuality rather

---

[115] Her husband was serving in the army in Italy. It is said that the book was widely read in messes and barracks in the last year of the war.

[116] L. Hall, *Hidden Anxieties*, 88; Holtzmann, 'Pursuit of Married Love', 41.

[117] Stocks in Box (ed.), *The Trial of Marie Stopes*, 9.

[118] See McKibbin, *Classes and Cultures*, 296–321.

[119] For the manuals as a genre, see R. Porter and L. Hall, *The Facts of Life*, 202–23.

than the liberation of women's sexuality as the goal of feminist sexual politics.[120] Stopes broke decisively with that tradition and, again, almost certainly to the satisfaction of her women readers.

Just how decisively can be seen by comparing the tone of *Married Love* with that of the most serious of the pre-First World War attempts to present sexual facts 'frankly' to a wide readership— Cassell's 'Question of Sex' series. These little books, most of which were published on the eve of the First World War, were written by the publicly acknowledged experts on sex: two of them by men cited in *Married Love*, Sir Thomas Clouston and Walter Heape, and another by a woman destined to be Stopes's perpetual sparring partner, Dr (later Dame) Mary Scharlieb, a very powerful doctor indeed. The introduction to the series by its general editor, F. B. Meyer, seems helpful enough:

The policy of evading, with silly and misleading answers, the natural curiosity of young people about their origin has been tried for generations with disastrous results. What has been the result of this policy of silence about the primal facts of life? What are the fruits that have resulted from the reticence of parents, teachers and others, the vast accumulation of quackery, of bad literature, of dishonoured lives, wrecked homes, and untimely graves, must answer.[121]

In fact, it is hard to imagine books more ill-judged to serve Meyer's purpose. They are driven by the doctrine of fear. The language is one of degeneration, corruption, and decay; the nightmare of disease; the sexual hopelessness of youths with an 'artistic temperament'; the eugenic catastrophe facing the race; and the racial necessity of control and restraint.[122] Marriage was not depicted as joyful, nor sex as ecstatic. Rather, marriage was a sacrifice for the future of

---

[120] See Holtzmann, 'Pursuit of Married Love', 41; Soloway, *Birth Control and the Population Question*, 209–10; McKibbin, *Classses and Cultures*, 297. There was, of course, an alternative, though not predominant, feminist tradition. For this see M. Joannou, 'The Angel of Freedom: Dora Marsden and the transformation of *The Free-woman* into *The Egoist*', *Women's History Review*, 11/4 (2002), 601–2. Within the social purity movement there was also an anti-ascetic argument not altogether different from Stopes's own. See e.g. S. Morgan, *A Passion for Purity: Ellice Hopkins and the politics of gender in the Late-Victorian church* (Bristol, 1999), 147–54.

[121] F. B. Meyer in T. Clouston, *Before I Wed or Young Men and Marriage* (London, 1913), pp. viii–ix.

[122] See as examples: ibid. 40, 53, 67–9, 70–7; M. Scharlieb, *What it Means to Marry; or Young Women and Marriage* (London, 1914), 86, 114–19, 135–7.

the race in which women were offered a role Stopes specifically repudiated in *Married Love*. Walter Heape wrote that he had

no hesitation in saying that after puberty hard games and hard brain work are inimical to the development of those special qualities which are essential to the efficient discharge of the maternal duties nature designed women to perform . . . Such duty should overwhelm all individual desires for ease and luxury, for freedom from subsequent cares and risk of onerous ties. The nation demands this sacrifice of women, if indeed it be a sacrifice; it demands that she shall put aside that selfishness which so often stands in the way of her performing maternal duties, while nature, by the supreme happiness it confers on the mother, thus pays for that sacrifice.[123]

In the case of Mary Scharlieb, her book is driven by an almost sadistically punitive Christianity. Of the proposal, for instance, that divorce be permissible on grounds of insanity, she wrote:

It is just possible to imagine that, where extreme violence of temper occurs in an individual who inflames himself or herself by the intemperate use of alcohol, continued cohabitation might be rendered extremely difficult, perhaps impossible, but, taking it at its worst, a violent temper with quasi-insane outbreaks of rage can do nothing to nullify the marriage vow. This great misfortune may be turned into a blessing and accepted as a means of discipline; it may become the painful but purifying agent whereby character is developed and moral strength attained.[124]

Stopes herself, of course, agreed with much of this. She too feared for the future of the race and was unsympathetic to divorce. But the spirit of *Married Love* is a world away from Cassell's. It is one of love, companionship, and pleasure. And also secular. Stopes was certainly not hostile to religion as such—the reverse if anything— and was careful not to alienate religious opinion more than she had to; but as a received system of ethics it was not important in her writing. Thus the formidable religious injunctions which dominate the work of Scharlieb *et al.* are absent in *Married Love*. Since, furthermore (unlike the Cassell's authors, who were all opposed to contraception), she believed the future of the race lay in quality rather than number, she could advocate marriage unencumbered by redundant children with a good conscience. Which is what the middle

---

[123] W. Heape, *Preparation for Marriage* (London, 1914), 87–9. See also his comments on the 'bright hardness' of girls educated at Newnham and Girton Colleges, Cambridge (p. 133). Heape was a fellow of Trinity College, Cambridge.

[124] Scharlieb, *What it Means to Marry*, 82–3.

classes, and, soon, the working classes, wanted to hear. We must remember that *Married Love* was published when the British birth rate was falling rapidly. In advocating contraception Stopes was not advocating something people were not practising. The only explanation for Britain's declining fertility from the last quarter of the nineteenth century onwards is that people were consciously limiting the size of their families. *Married Love* was popular because, *inter alia*, it gave an acceptable rationale to what people were doing anyway. She was on the side of history: the Cassell's authors were arguing against it.

Stopes's strategy in the writing of *Married Love* added to its success. As we have seen, she was careful not to turn a book certain to be shocking into one certain to be scandalous. By asserting her personal adherence to monogamous marriage and extramarital chastity (not something she invariably supported), and her opposition to abortion, she made her form of married love acceptable to those who would have been alienated by anything 'immoral'. As Richard Soloway has argued, *Married Love* 'readily appealed to a new generation of women after the [first world] war and offered a compromise to sensitive, intelligent men worried about the reconciliation of feminist independence with the traditional maintenance of the family and the race'.[125] That the book was not characteristic of Stopes's writing as a whole made it the more acceptable. Eugenics scarcely appears at all and birth control—despite the notoriety of Chapter IX—almost as an afterthought; which eliminated the two themes of her later writing some found most offputting. *Married Love* is a book of marriage guidance, and about the art of love within marriage, not a book (unlike *Wise Parenthood*) about racial health or the technology of family planning—though it assumes the planned family is necessary for marital happiness.

The morality of the book is, above all, conventional. Although Stopes abandoned the idea of writing *Married Love* as a series of romantic novels, it is nevertheless a romance: as much a romance as *Pride and Prejudice* or a Mills and Boon novel. It is about love and the ideal marriage; the oldest plot in English literature. What Jane Austen or a Mills and Boon author do not tell their readers, of course, is that there is a physical sexual reality to marriage, an art

---

[125] Soloway, *Birth Control and the Population Question*, 211–12.

which must be learnt if the marriage is indeed to be ideal: falling in love is not enough. Once that is admitted, however, *Married Love* comes within the canon of the romantic novel, as Stopes would have wanted. It was popular precisely because it catered for most people's idea of what marriage should be. That there is a real feminist sting in the tail—the penultimate chapter—probably passed most readers by: its argument was too implicit and depended too much upon life chances not available even then to the majority of middle-class women.

It had become clear by the end of 1918 that Stopes's interests were moving from marriage guidance to birth control; from the middle to the working classes. Some did not like this. Bernard Shaw told her that she really was 'a matrimonial expert, which is something much wider and more needed than a specialist in contraception. You should make it clear that you are a doctor, not a Malthusian nor a trader in sterilizing devices.'[126] This was not advice she was inclined to take. She became more political, more combative, more intolerant. Her personal vanity teetered into egomania. She was increasingly difficult to work with and increasingly marginalized—because so difficult to work with—even in the birth-control movement. Her marriage, in effect, broke up.[127] After the Second World War her relations with her son became very strained. She was ever more cranky in her views. This is well known. Yet she always had courage. It took courage to write *Married Love*, however conventional its morality. It took courage to argue the case for birth-control as she did. It took courage to take on such formidable opponents as the Roman Catholic Church and polite opinion. And she had a sense of the way society was evolving; how futile it was to resist social evolution— though this did not mean that evolution could not be given a firm push. In the public mind she is now regarded as one of the most significant British women of the twentieth century. It was this courage and sense of history, together with flamboyance and egoistic self-confidence, a combination often very damaging in her private life, that made her so.

[126] Rose, *Marie Stopes*, 193.
[127] For this rather miserable episode, see ibid. 198–237.

SELECT BIBLIOGRAPHY

This is not an exhaustive bibliography, but is designed to give the reader the more immediately useful literature on *Married Love*. More detailed literature can be found in the Introduction.

Works by Marie Stopes

Married Love (1st edn. London, 1918).
Married Love (7th edn. London, 1919).
Wise Parenthood (London, 1918).
Radiant Motherhood (London, 1920).
Enduring Passion (London, 1928).

The above are a 'series' of which *Married Love* is the first. P. Eaton and M. Warwick, *Marie Stopes: A Checklist of her Writings* (London, 1977) gives a publishing history of *Married Love*.

Biographies of Marie Stopes

K. Briant, *Marie Stopes: A Biography* (London, 1962) (although Briant was very close to Stopes his book is informative and not uncritical).

R. Hall, *Marie Stopes: A Biography* (London, 1977).

A. Maude, *Marie Stopes: Her Work and Play* (London, ?1933) (written very much under Stopes's influence, but it contains some helpful material).

J. Rose, *Marie Stopes and the Sexual Revolution* (London, 1992).

Useful Secondary Literature

M. Box (ed.), *The Trial of Marie Stopes* (London, 1967) (a transcript of the libel action before the High Court Stopes took against Dr Halliday Sutherland; mainly about birth control, but interesting on the origins of *Married Love*).

P. Grosskurth, *Havelock Ellis: A Biography* (New York, 1985).

Lesley A. Hall, 'Marie Stopes and Her Correspondents: Personalising Population Decline in an Era of Demographic Change', in R. A. Peel (ed.), *Marie Stopes and the English Birth Control Movement* (London, 1997).

—— *Hidden Anxieties: Male Sexuality, 1900–1950* (London, 1991).

R. Hall (ed.), *Dear Dr Stopes: Sex in the 1920s* (London, 1978) (a selection from the correspondence Stopes received from 1918 on; very informative (and often entertaining)).

Ellen M. Holtzmann, 'The Pursuit of Married Love: Women's Attitudes toward Sexuality and Marriage in Great Britain, 1918–1939', *Journal of Social History*, 16/2 (Winter 1982) (very helpful and also draws on Stopes's correspondence).

J. Lewis, *Women in England 1870–1950* (Brighton, 1984).

J. Peel, 'Contraception and the Medical Profession', *Population Studies* 18/2 (Nov. 1964).

R. Porter and Lesley A. Hall, *The Facts of Life: The Creation of Sexual Knowledge in Britain (1650–1950)* (New Haven and London, 1995) (the best introduction to the subject).

R. A. Soloway, *Birth Control and the Population Question in England, 1877–1930* (Chapel Hill, NC, and London, 1982).

—— 'The Galton Lecture 1996: Marie Stopes, Eugenics and the Birth Control Movement', in Peel (ed.), *Marie Stopes, Eugenics and the English Birth Control Movement*.

J. Weeks, *Sex, Politics and Society* (2nd edn. London and New York, 1989) (a very good discussion of Stopes within the wider social and political history of sexuality).

Further Reading in Oxford World's Classics

Charlotte Perkins Gilman, *The Yellow Wall-Paper and Other Stories*, ed. Robert Shulman.

Kamasutra, trans. and ed. Wendy Doniger and Sudhir Kakar.

A CHRONOLOGY OF MARIE STOPES

1880 Born on 15 October in Edinburgh to Charlotte Carmichael Stopes and Henry Stopes.

1892 Day Student at St George's High School Edinburgh.

1894 Becomes a student at North London Collegiate School when her parents move to London.

1900 Undergraduate at University College London.

1902 Graduates with first-class honours in botany and third-class honours in geology. Death of her father in December.

1904 Awarded her Ph.D. at the University of Munich. There meets Kenjiro Fujii. Appointed demonstrator in botany at the University of Manchester.

1905 Awarded her D.Sc.

1907–8 In Japan to study plant fossils. The relationship with Fujii finally fails.

1909 Appointed lecturer in botany at the University of Manchester.

1910–11 Resigns from the University of Manchester; goes to Canada to study carboniferous flora. Meets and marries Reginald Ruggles Gates. Returns to England.

1912–13 Meets Aylmer Maude who moves in with Stopes and Gates as a lodger.

1914 Gates forces Maude to leave the house. In May Stopes leaves Gates and in October files for nullity. After a series of false starts she drafts what becomes *Married Love*.

1916 Marriage to Gates annulled on grounds of non-consummation. Gates does not contest the action.

1917 *Married Love* completed.

1918 *Married Love* published by A. C. Fifield in March; instantly successful. Stopes meets Humphrey Verdon Roe, who subsidizes the publication of *Married Love*. Marries Roe in May. *Wise Parenthood* published in December. Also an instant success.

1919 Birth of her first child, Henry, stillborn. Seventh edition of *Married Love* published in May by G. P. Putnam's Sons.

1920 Publication of *Radiant Motherhood*.

1921 Queens Hall meeting in favour of birth control (31 May).

Stopes and Roe open their first birth-control clinic in Holloway. The Society for Constructive Birth Control founded, with Stopes as president and Roe as secretary.

1923   Begins libel action (which she eventually loses) against Dr Halliday Sutherland.

1924   Birth of her second son, Harry.

1928   Publication of *Enduring Passion* and her first novel, *Love's Creation*. Sued for libel by the editor of the *Morning Post* and Halliday Sutherland.

1929   Death of her mother in February.

1939   Falls in love with Keith Briant. Marriage clearly failing; Stopes and Roe now effectively separated.

1949   Death of Humphrey Verdon Roe in July.

1957   Diagnosed as having breast cancer.

1958   Dies on 2 October.

MARRIED LOVE

A New Contribution to the Solution of Sex Difficulties

MARIE CARMICHAEL STOPES

Doctor of Science, London; Doctor of Philosophy, Munich; Fellow of University College, London; Fellow of the Royal Society of Literature, and the Linnean Society, London

With a Preface by Dr JESSIE MURRAY and LETTERS from PROFESSOR E. H. STARLING, FRS, and FATHER STANISLAUS ST JOHN, SJ

Dedicated to young husbands and
all those who are betrothed in love

CONTENTS

PREFACE

by MISS JESSIE MURRAY,* MB, BS

IN this little book Dr Marie Stopes deals with subjects which are generally regarded as too sacred for an entirely frank treatment. Some earnest and delicate minds may feel apprehensive that such frankness in details is 'dangerous,' because the effect on prurient minds might be to give them food for their morbid fancies. It is just such a fear which has been largely responsible for the silence and mystery which have for so long been wrapped round the sacred rites of mating.

The question now is, Has this reticence been carried too far? Has it been carried so far that it now tends to defeat its purpose of safeguarding public morals? There are many who unhesitatingly answer such questions in the affirmative. Their intimate knowledge of human lives compels them to recognise that at least as much harm is done by silence as by speaking out. Everything depends on how the matter is presented.

Those who are shocked at the publication of such a book as this on the ground that it gives material for impure minds to sport with, need only reflect that such material is already amply provided in certain comic papers, in hosts of inferior novels, too often on the stage and film, and presented thus in coarse and demoralising guise. It can do nothing but good to such minds to meet the facts they are already so familiar with in a totally new light.

On the other hand, there are all the earnest and noble young minds who seek to know what responsibilities they are taking on themselves when they marry, and how they may best meet these responsibilities. How few of them have more than the vaguest ideas on the subject! How few of them know how or where to obtain the help they desire!

They recoil from the coarse and impure sources of information which are so accessible, and they hesitate to approach those they have learned to regard as virtuous and modest, realising that from such they will receive so little actual information, and that so veiled as to be almost useless.

Dr Stopes has attempted to meet the need of such seekers, and her book will certainly be warmly welcomed by them. It is calculated to prevent many of those mistakes which wreck the happiness of countless lovers as soon as they are actually married. If it did no more than this it would be valuable indeed!

But there is an even more important aspect to be considered— the effect on the child. In all civilised lands there is a growing sense of responsibility towards the young.

The problems of their physical and mental nurture attract more and more attention day by day. Eugenists, educationists, physicians, politicians, philanthropists, and even ordinary parents discuss and ponder, ponder and discuss matters both great and small which have a bearing on the development of the child. By common consent the first seven years of life are regarded as the most critical. It is during these years that the foundations of the personality-to-be are laid—'well and truly' or otherwise. It is during these years that the deepest and most ineradicable impressions are made in the plastic constitution of the child, arresting or developing this or the other instinctive trend and fixing it, often for life.

And it is during these years above all that the parents play the most important rôle in the inner history of the child's life, not so much by anything they directly teach through verbal exhortations, warnings, or commands, as by those subtler influences which are conveyed in gesture, tone, and facial expression. The younger the child, the more is it influenced through these more primitive modes of expression, and quite as much when they are not directed towards itself but are employed by the parents in their intimate relations with one another in the presence of their apparently unobserving child—the infant in its cot, the toddling baby by the hearth, the little child to all appearance absorbed in its picture book or toy.

Is it not of the utmost importance that these earliest impressions should be of the finest nature? And should we not therefore welcome all that may help—as this book can—to make the living cradle of the next generation as full of beauty and harmony as love and mutual understanding can?

The age-long conflict between the 'lower' and the 'higher' impulses, between the primitive animal nature and the specifically human developments of an altruistic and ethical order, are fought afresh in each soul and in every marriage.

We need to realise more clearly that the lower is never—ought never to be—*eliminated* but rather *subsumed by the higher*. No true harmony can be hoped for so long as one factor or the other is ignored or repressed.

Dr Stopes makes some very important biological suggestions which should not be lightly dismissed. Further observation is required to establish or disprove her theory of the normal sexual cycle in women, but my own observation certainly tends to confirm it.

J. M. MURRAY

LETTER

from Professor E. H. STARLING,* MD, BS, FRS
Professor of Physiology, University of London

UNIVERSITY COLLEGE,
GOWER STREET, LONDON, WC,
November 23, 1917.

DEAR DR STOPES,—

The need of such guidance as you give is very evident. After all, instinct in man is all insufficient to determine social behaviour, and there is need of instruction in the highest of physiological functions, that of reproduction, as there is in the lower functions of eating and drinking—the only difference being that in the former instruction can be deferred to a later age. And there is no doubt that in this case it is better to acquire knowledge by instruction than by a type of experience which is nearly always sordid and may be fraught with danger to the health of the individual and of the family.

At the present time it is of vital importance to the State that its marriages should be fruitful—in children, happiness, and efficiency (and all three are closely connected).

If your book helps in securing this object, your trouble will not have been in vain.

Believe me,
Yours very truly,
ERNEST H. STARLING

AUTHOR'S PREFACE

MORE than ever to-day are happy homes needed. It is my hope that this book may serve the State by adding to their numbers. Its object is to increase the joys of marriage, and to show how much sorrow may be avoided.

The only secure basis for a present-day State is the welding of its units in marriage; but there is rottenness and danger at the foundations of the State if many of the marriages are unhappy. To-day, particularly in the middle classes in this country, marriage is far less really happy than its surface appears. Too many who marry expecting joy are bitterly disappointed; and the demand for 'freedom' grows; while those who cry aloud are generally unaware that it is more likely to have been their own ignorance than the 'marriage-bond' which was the origin of their unhappiness.

It is never *easy* to make marriage a lovely thing; and it is an achievement beyond the powers of the selfish, or the mentally cowardly. Knowledge is needed and, as things are at present, knowledge is almost unobtainable by those who are most in want of it.

The problems of the sex-life are infinitely complex, and for their solution urgently demand both sympathy and scientific research.

I have some things to say about sex, which, so far as I am aware, have not yet been said, things which seem to be of profound importance to men and women who hope to make their marriages beautiful.

This little book is less a record of a research than an attempt to present in easily understandable form the clarified and crystallised results of long and complex investigations. Its simple statements are based on a very large number of first-hand observations, on confidences from men and women of all classes and types, and on facts gleaned from wide reading.

My original contributions to the age-long problems of

marriage will principally be found in Chapters IV, V, and VIII. The other chapters fill in what I hope is an undistorted picture of the potential beauties and realities of marriage.

The whole is written simply, and for the ordinary untrained reader, though it embodies some observations which will be new even to those who have made scientific researches on the subjects of sex and human physiology. These observations I intend to supplement and publish at greater length and in more scientific language in another place.

I do not now touch upon the many human variations and abnormalities which bulk so largely in most books on sex, nor do I deal with the many problems raised by incurably unhappy marriages.

In the following pages I speak to those—and in spite of all our neurotic literature and plays they are in the great majority—who are nearly normal, and who are married or about to be married, and hope, but do not know how, to make their marriages beautiful and happy.

To the reticent, as to the conventional, it may seem a presumption or a superfluity to speak of the details of the most complex of all our functions. They ask: Is not instinct enough? The answer is No. Instinct is *not* enough. In every other human activity it has been realised that training, the handing on of tradition are essential. As Dr Saleeby* once wisely pointed out: A cat knows how to manage her new-born kittens, how to bring them up and teach them; a human mother does not know how to manage her baby unless she is trained, either directly or by her own quick observation of other mothers. A cat performs her simple duties by instinct; a human mother has to be trained to fulfil her very complex ones.

The same is true in the subtle realm of sex. In this country, in modern times, the old traditions, the profound primitive knowledge of the needs of both sexes have been lost, and nothing but a muffled confusion of individual gossip disturbs a silence, shame-faced or foul. Here and there, in a family of fine tradition, a youth or maiden may learn some of the mysteries of marriage, but the great majority of people in our country have no glimmering of the supreme human art, the art of love; while in books on advanced Physiology and Medicine the gaps, the omissions, and even the misstatements of bare fact are amazing.

In my own marriage I paid such a terrible price for sex-ignorance that I feel that knowledge gained at such a cost should be placed at the service of humanity. In this little book average, healthy, mating creatures will find the key to the happiness which should be the portion of each. It has already guided some to happiness, and I hope it may save some others years of heartache and blind questioning in the dark.

MARIE CARMICHAEL STOPES

LETTER

from Father STANISLAUS ST JOHN,* SJ, CF

114, MOUNT STREET,
LONDON, W1,
December 11, 1917.

DEAR DR STOPES

I have read 'Married Love' with deep interest. As a piece of thoughtful, scientific writing I find it admirable throughout, and it seems to me that your theme could not have been treated in more beautiful or more delicate language, or with a truer ring of sympathy for those who, through ignorance or want of thought, make shipwreck of their married happiness.

Your clear exposition of the rhythmic curve of sex-feeling and of the misinterpretation on the part of so many husbands of what they call their wives' contrariness, arising from their ignorance of its existence, should bring happiness to many married couples whose lives are drifting apart through want of knowledge. In the exercise of my ministry I have repeatedly traced the beginnings of the rift to this want of knowledge and consequently of sympathy.

So far we are in complete agreement, but our ways part when you treat of birth control.

You write primarily as a scientist (though a very human scientist), and so you are naturally mainly occupied with the facts and conditions of what I may call our earth-life. I, on the other hand, writing as a Catholic, regard our earth-life as essentially and inseparably connected with an eternal existence which reaches out beyond the grave. I look on this life as utterly meaningless in itself, as a period which is simply and solely a means to an end— Eternity—a period of which all the circumstances of pleasure and pain can only be explained and rightly used in their relation to this Eternity.

Let me take in illustration of my meaning the case you give of the worn-out mother of twelve. The Catholic belief is that the loss of health on her part for a few years of life and the diminished vitality on the part of her later children would be a very small price indeed to pay for an endless happiness on the part of all.

In our belief, then, the destruction of one spermatazoon is not the question, but the deliberate prevention of an eternally happy existence which, in the supposition, might arise from its preservation. Holding, as we do, that the marriage-act is the divinely ordained means by which man offers to God the opportunity of creating an immortal being, we do not believe that he may make use of this means and deliberately frustrate it of its end without doing grave wrong.

You do me the honour of suggesting that I should write a foreword to your book, but any foreword from me could obviously only derive value from my position as a Catholic priest, and that position is in opposition to this part of your work.

I cannot end without thanking you very sincerely for allowing me to read your book. Apart from what, as a Catholic, I object to in it, it contains so much most helpful matter that I feel sure it will bring to many a happiness in married life now wanting through the ignorance and the consequent want of sympathy which you so rightly deplore.

Believe me, dear Dr Stopes,
Yours very sincerely,
S. St John, SJ, CF

I publish this letter with sincere thanks to Father St John for his permission to use it.—M.C.S.

REPLY

to Father St John, sj

Dear Father St John

Your letter wins my heart entirely by its appreciation and kindness. It is a great help and encouragement to find that we are so far in essential agreement, and that you are so well disposed toward even part of my effort.

But—and I wish I could say it in burning words—it is not because I am chiefly concerned with Time that I wrote Chapter IX, but just because I am so acutely and so persistently conscious that I am dealing with factors of Eternity. *To me to-day is essentially a part of my Life Everlasting.*

I cannot separate time and eternity, this world and the next, as religious people often seem able to do; to me this body is a tool in the service of (though not completely in the control of) my immortal soul. Now it seems to me that religious people—and even in your letter I fancy I detect the same tendency (forgive me if I am wrong)—are too ready to separate this world and the next, to act unreasonably or cruelly here and to trust to Eternity, or the Hereafter, to put all right. I do not think that is the way God wills us to work out His plans now that He is giving us the knowledge to do better.

Could there be anything more unreasonable or cruel than to bring into life half a dozen children *doomed from birth* to ill-health, poverty, and almost inevitable crime?

Christ forgave the thief upon the Cross, but He said, 'Woe unto him through whom offences come. It were better for him that a millstone were hanged about his neck and he cast into the sea.' Would Christ approve of deliberately creating a thief by bringing forth a child who was one inevitably through predictable weakness of physique and mentality and an environment of poverty? ('Thief' stands for criminals in general.)

But more, what about others, born dead, born imbecile, thwarted of life by miscarriage, which tear and rend the over-burdened mother so that she is forced to neglect the children she has, and her neglect turns them into thieves? The poor, uneducated mother commits this crime through ignorance: it is *we who know* and allow her to remain in ignorance who are really responsible. Is not our withholding God-given knowledge the greatest stumbling-block of offence to these little ones, and shall we not deserve the millstone round our necks?

Were everyone to have all the children physiologically possible (now that infant mortality is so much reduced by science) in a few centuries there would not be standing room on the earth, and nowhere for a blade of grass or an ear of corn to grow between the crowding feet. Is then a Roman Catholic mother, the increases to whose large family get punier and punier, to be privileged to go deliberately with that host of puny children *at the expense of others*, not only through that part of Eternity called Time, but through all Eternity?

But, dear Father St John, it is not my place to preach or to argue with you, especially after your generous kindness and appreciation. And, alas! I fully realise that even were I granted the tongues of men and of angels, and I converted you to my thought in this matter, you as a Roman Catholic priest could not uphold a position in opposition to your Church.

Oh, that the Churches would look to Christ's own words instead of to the official Church interpretation of them!

I thank you very sincerely for your kindness to a stranger, and remain, always yours respectfully,

MARIE CARMICHAEL STOPES

CHAPTER I

THE HEART'S DESIRE

She gave him comprehension of the meaning of love: a word in
many mouths, not often explained. With her, wound in his idea
of her, he perceived it to signify a new start in our existence, a
finer shoot of the tree stoutly planted in good gross earth; the
senses running their live sap, and the minds companioned, and
the spirits made one by the whole-natured conjunction. In
sooth, a happy prospect for the sons and daughters of Earth,
divinely indicating more than happiness: the speeding of us,
compact of what we are, between the ascetic rocks and the
sensual whirlpools, to the creation of certain nobler races, nor
very dimly imagined.—GEORGE MEREDITH's 'Diana of the
Crossways,' chap. 37.

EVERY heart desires a mate. For some reason beyond our comprehension, nature has so created us that we are incomplete in
ourselves; neither man nor woman singly can know the joy of the
performance of all the human functions; neither man nor woman
singly can create another human being. This fact, which is
expressed in our outward divergencies of form, influences and
colours the whole of our lives; and there is nothing for which the
innermost spirit of one and all so yearns as for a sense of union
with another soul, and the perfecting of oneself which such union
brings.

In all young people, unless they have inherited depraved or
diseased faculties, the old desire of our race springs up afresh in
its pristine beauty.

With the dreams and bodily changes of adolescence, come to
the youth and maiden the strange and powerful impulses of the
racial instinct. The bodily differences of the two, now accentuated, become mystical, alluring, enchanting in their promise.
Their differences unite and hold together the man and the
woman so that their bodily union is the solid nucleus of an
immense fabric of interwoven strands reaching to the uttermost
ends of the earth; some lighter than the filmiest cobweb, or than

the softest wave of music, iridescent with the colours, not only of the visible rainbow, but of all the invisible glories of the wave-lengths of the soul.

However much he may conceal it under assumed cynicism, worldliness, or self-seeking, the heart of every young man yearns with a great longing for the fulfilment of the beautiful dream of a lifelong union with a mate. Each heart knows instinctively that it is only a mate who can give full comprehension of all the potential greatness in the soul, and have tender laughter for all the child-like wonder that lingers so enchantingly even in the white-haired.

The search for a mate is a quest for an understanding heart clothed in a body beautiful, but unlike our own.

In the modern world, those who set out on high endeavours or who consciously separate themselves from the ordinary course of social life, are comparatively few, and it is not to them that I am speaking. The great majority of our citizens—both men and women—after a time of waiting, or of exploring, or of oscillating from one attraction to another, 'settle down' and marry.

Very few are actually so cynical as to marry without the hope of happiness; while most young people, however their words may deny it and however they may conceal their tender hopes by an assumption of cynicism, reveal that they are conscious of entering on a new and glorious state by their radiant looks and the joyous buoyancy of their actions. In the kisses and the hand touch of the betrothed are a zest and exhilaration which stir the blood like wine. The two read poetry, listen entranced to music which echoes the songs of their pulses, and see reflected in each other's eyes the beauty of the world. In the midst of this celestial intoxication they naturally assume that, as they are on the threshold of their lives, so too they are in but the ante-chamber of their experience of spiritual unity.

The more sensitive, the more romantic, and the more idealistic is the young person of either sex, the more his or her soul craves for some kindred soul with whom the whole being can unite. But all have some measure of this desire, even the most prosaic, and we know from innumerable stories of real life that the sternest man of affairs, he who may have worldly success of every sort, may yet, through the lack of a real mate, live with a sense almost as though the limbs of his soul had been amputated. Edward Carpenter* has beautifully voiced this longing:—

That there should exist one other person in the world towards whom all openness of interchange should establish itself, from whom there should be no concealment; whose body should be as dear to one, in every part, as one's own; with whom there should be no sense of Mine or Thine, in property or possession; into whose mind one's thoughts should naturally flow, as it were to know themselves and to receive a new illumination; and between whom and oneself there should be a spontaneous rebound of sympathy in all the joys and sorrows and experiences of life; such is perhaps one of the dearest wishes of the soul.—'Love's Coming of Age.'

It may chance that someone into whose hands this book falls may protest that he or she has never felt the fundamental yearning to form a part of that trinity which alone is the perfect expression of humanity. If that is so, it is possible that all unconsciously he may be suffering from a real malady—sex anaesthesia. This is the name given to an inherent coldness, which, while it lacks the usual human impulse of tenderness, is generally quite unconscious of its lack. It may even be that the reader's departure from the ordinary ranks of mankind is still more fundamental, in which case, instead of sitting in judgment on the majority, he will do well to read some such book as 'The Sexual Question' (English translation 1908) by the famous Professor August Forel,* in order that his own nature may be made known to him. He may then discover to which type of our widely various humanity he belongs. He need not read my book, for it is written about, and it is written for, ordinary men and women who, feeling themselves incomplete, yearn for a union that will have power not only to make a fuller and richer thing of their own lives, but which will place them in a position to use their sacred trust as creators of lives to come.

It has happened many times in human history that individuals have not only been able to conquer this natural craving for a mate, but have set up celibacy as a higher ideal. In its most beautiful expression and sublimest manifestations, the celibate ideal has proclaimed a world-wide love, in place of the narrower human love of home and children. Many saints and sages, reformers and dogmatists have modelled their lives on this ideal. But such individuals cannot be taken as the standard of the *race*, for they are out of its main current: they are branches which may flower, but never fruit in a bodily form.

In this world our spirits not only permeate matter but find their only expression through its medium. So long as we are human we must have bodies, and bodies obey chemical and physiological, as well as spiritual laws.

If our race as a whole set out to pursue an ideal which must ultimately eliminate bodies altogether, it is clear that very soon we should find the conditions of our environment so altered that we could no longer speak of the human race.

In the meantime, we *are* human. We each and all live our lives according to laws, some of which we have begun to understand, many of which are completely hidden from us. The most complete human being is he or she who consciously or unconsciously obeys the profound physical laws of our being in such a way that the spirit receives as much help and as little hindrance from the body as possible. A mind and spirit finds its fullest expression thwarted by the misuse, neglect or gross abuse of the body in which it dwells.

By the ignorant or self-indulgent breaking of fundamental laws endless harmonies are dislocated. The modern, small-minded ascetic endeavours to grow spiritually by destroying his physical instincts instead of by using them. But I would proclaim that we are set in the world so to mould matter that it may express our spirits; that it is presumption to profess to fight the immemorial laws of our physical being, and that he who does so loses unconsciously the finest flux in which wondrous new creations take their rise.

To use a homely simile—one might compare two human beings to two bodies charged with electricity of different potentials. Isolated from each other the electric forces within them are invisible, but if they come into the right juxtaposition the force is transmuted, and a spark, a glow of burning light arises between them. Such is love.

From the body of the loved one's simple, sweetly coloured flesh, which our immemorial creature instincts urge us to desire, there springs not only the wonder of a new bodily life, but also the enlargement of the horizon of human sympathy and the glow of spiritual understanding which a solitary soul could never have attained alone.

Many reading this may feel conscious that they have had physical union without such spiritual results, perhaps even without an accession of ordinary happiness. If that is so, it can only be because, consciously or unconsciously, they have broken some of the profound laws which govern the love of man and woman. Only by learning to hold a bow correctly can one draw music from a violin: only by obedience to the laws of the lower plane can one step up to the plane above.

CHAPTER II

THE BROKEN JOY

What shall be done to quiet the heart-cry of the world? How answer the dumb appeal for help we so often divine below eyes that laugh?—AE in 'The Hero in Man.'*

DREAMING of happiness, feeling that at last they have each found the one who will give eternal understanding and tenderness, the young man and maiden marry.[1]

At first, in the time generally called the honeymoon, the unaccustomed freedom and the sweetness of the relation often does bring real happiness. How long does it last? Too often a far shorter time than is generally acknowledged.

In the first joy of their union it is hidden from the two young people that they know little or nothing about the fundamental laws of each other's being. Much of the sex-attraction (not only among human beings, but even throughout the whole world of living creatures) depends upon the differences between the two that pair; and probably taking them all unawares, those very differences which drew them together now begin to work their undoing.

But so long as the first illusion that each understands the other is supported by the thrilling delight of ever-fresh discoveries, the sensations lived through are so rapid and so joyous that the lovers do not realise that there is no firm foundation of real mutual knowledge beneath their feet. While even the happiest pair may know of divergencies about religion, politics, social custom, and opinions on things in general, these, with goodwill, patience, and intelligence on either side, can be ultimately adjusted, because in all such things there is a common meeting ground for the two. Human beings, while differing widely about every conceivable

[1] In this, and in most of the generalisations found in this book, I am speaking of things as they are in Great Britain. While, to a considerable extent, the same is true of America and the Scandinavian countries, it must be remembered all through that I am speaking of the British and primarily of our educated classes.

subject in such human relations, have at least *thought* about them, threshed them out, and discussed them openly for generations.

But about the much more fundamental and vital problems of sex, there is a lack of knowledge so abysmal and so universal that its mists and shadowy darkness have affected even the few who lead us, and who are prosecuting research in these subjects. And the two young people begin to suffer from fundamental divergencies, before perhaps they realise that such exist, and with little prospect of ever gaining a rational explanation of them.

Nearly all those whose own happiness seems to be dimmed or broken count themselves exceptions, and comfort themselves with the thought of some of their friends, who, they feel sure, have attained the happiness which they themselves have missed.

It is generally supposed that happy people, like happy nations, have no history—they are silent about their own affairs. Those who talk about their marriage are generally those who have missed the happiness they expected. True as this may be in general, it is not permanently and profoundly true, and there are people who are reckoned, and still reckon themselves, happy, but who yet unawares reveal the secret disappointment which clouds their inward peace.

Leaving out of account '*femmes incomprises*'* and all the innumerable neurotic, super-sensitive, and slightly abnormal people, it still remains an astonishing and tragic fact that *so* large a proportion of marriages lose their early bloom and are to some extent unhappy.

For years many men and women have confided to me the secrets of their lives; and of all the innumerable marriages of which the inner circumstances are known to me, there are tragically few which approach even humanly attainable joy.

Many of those considered by the world, by the relatives, *even by the loved and loving partner*, to be perfectly happy marriages, are secretly shadowed to the more sensitive of the pair.

Where the bride is, as are so many of our educated girls, composed of virgin sweetness shut in ignorance, the man is often the first to create 'the rift within the lute'; but his suffering begins almost simultaneously with hers. The surface freedom of our women has not materially altered, cannot materially alter, the pristine purity of a girl of our northern race. She generally has not even the capacity to imagine the basic facts of physical marriage, and her bridegroom may shock her without knowing that he was doing so. Then, unconscious of the nature, and even perhaps of the existence of his fault, he is bewildered and pained by her inarticulate pain.

Yet I think, nevertheless, it is true that in the early days of marriage the young man is often even more sensitive, more romantic, more easily pained about all ordinary things, and he enters marriage hoping for an even higher degree of spiritual and bodily unity than does the girl or the woman. But the man is more quickly blunted, more swiftly rendered cynical, and is readier to look upon happiness as a Utopian dream than is his mate.

On the other hand, the woman is slower to realise disappointment, and more often by the sex-life of marriage is of the two the more *profoundly* wounded, with a slow corrosive wound that eats into her very being.

Perfect happiness is a unity composed of a myriad essences; and this one supreme thing is exposed to the attacks of countless destructive factors.

Were I to touch upon all the possible sources of marital disappointment and unhappiness, this book would expand into a dozen bulky volumes. As I am addressing those who I assume have read, or can read, other books written upon various ramifications of the subject, I will not discuss the themes which have been handled by many writers, nor deal with abnormalities, which fill so large a part of most books on sex.

In the last few years there has been such an awakening to the realisation of the corrosive horror of all aspects of prostitution that there is no need to labour the point that no marriage can be happy where the husband has, in buying another body, sold his own health with his honour, and is tainted with disease.

Nor is it necessary, in speaking to well-meaning, optimistic young couples, to enlarge upon the obvious dangers of drunkenness, self-indulgence, and the cruder forms of selfishness. It is with the subtler infringements of the fundamental laws we have to deal. And the prime tragedy is that, as a rule, the two young people are both unaware of the existence of such decrees. Yet here, as elsewhere in Nature, the law breaker is punished whether he is aware of the existence of the law he breaks or not.

In the state of ignorance which so largely predominates to-day, the first sign that things are amiss between the two who thought they were entering paradise together, is generally a sense of loneliness, a feeling that the one who was expected to have all in common is outside some experience, some subtle delight, and fails to understand the needs of the loved one. Trivialities are often the first indicators of something which takes its roots unseen in the profoundest depths. The girl may sob for hours over something so trifling that she cannot even put into words its nature, while the young man, thinking that he had set out with his soul's beloved upon an adventure into celestial distances, may find himself apparently up against a barrier in her which appears as incomprehensible as it is frivolous.

Then, so strange is the mystical inter-relation between our bodies, our minds, and our souls, that for crimes committed in ignorance of the dual functions of the married pair, and the laws which harmonise them, the punishments are reaped on planes quite diverse, till new and ever new misunderstandings appear to spring spontaneously from the soil of their mutual contact. Gradually or swiftly each heart begins to hide a sense of boundless isolation. It may be urged that this statement is too sweeping. It is, however, based on innumerable actual lives. I have heard from women whose marriages are looked upon by all as the happiest possible expressions of human felicity, the details of secret pain of which they have allowed their husbands no inkling. Many men will know how they have hidden from their beloved wives a sense of dull disappointment, perhaps at her coldness in the marital embrace, or from the sense that there is in her something elusive which always evades their grasp!

This profound sense of misunderstanding finds readier expression in the cruder and more ordinary natures. The disappointment of the married is expressed not only in innumerable books and plays, but even in comic papers and all our daily gossip.

Now that so many 'movements' are abroad, folk on all sides are emboldened to express the opinion that it is marriage itself which is at fault. Many think that merely by loosening the bonds, and making it possible to start afresh with someone else, their lives would be made harmonious and happy. But often such reformers forget that he or she who knows nothing of the way to make marriage great and beautiful with one partner, is not likely to succeed with another. Only by a reverent study of the Art of Love can the beauty of its expression be realised in linked lives.

And even when once learnt the Art of Love takes *time* to practise. As Ellen Key* says, 'Love requires peace, love will dream; it cannot live upon the remnants of our time and our personality.'

There is no doubt that Love loses, in the haste and bustle of the modern turmoil, not only its charm and graces, but some of its vital essence. The evil results of the haste which so infests and poisons us are often felt much more by the woman than by the man. The over-stimulation of city life tends to 'speed up' the man's reactions, but to retard hers. To make matters worse, even for those who have leisure to spend on love-making, the opportunities for peaceful, romantic dalliance are less to-day in a city with its tubes and cinema shows than in woods and gardens where the pulling of rosemary or lavender may be the sweet excuse for the slow and profound mutual rousing of passion. Now physical passion, so swiftly stimulated in man, tends to override all else, and the untutored man seeks but one thing—the accomplishment of desire. The woman, for it is in her nature so to do, forgives the crudeness, but sooner or later her love revolts, probably in secret, and then for ever after, though she may command an outward tenderness, she has nothing within but scorn and loathing for the act which should have been a perpetually recurring entrancement.

So many people are now born and bred in artificial and false surroundings, that even the elementary fact that the acts of love should be *joyous* is unknown to them. A distinguished American doctor made this amazing statement: 'I do not believe mutual pleasure in the sexual act has any particular bearing on the happiness of life.' (Amer. Med. Assoc. Rep. 1900). This is, perhaps, an extreme case, yet so many distinguished medical men, gynecologists and physiologists, are either in ignorance or error regarding some of the profoundest facts of human sex-life, that it is not surprising that ordinary young couples, however hopeful, should break and destroy the joy that might have been their life-long crown.

CHAPTER III

WOMAN'S 'CONTRARINESS'

Oh! for that Being whom I can conceive to be in the world, though I shall not live to prove it. One to whom I might have recourse in all my Humours and Dispositions: in all my Distempers of Mind, visionary Causes of Mortification, and Fairy Dreams of Pleasure. I have been trying to train up a Lady or two for these good offices of Friendship, but hitherto I must not boast of my success.—HERRICK.*

WHAT is the fate of the average man who marries, happily and hopefully, a girl well suited to him? He desires with his whole heart a mutual, life-long happiness. He marries with the intention of fulfilling every injunction given him by father, doctor, and friend. He is considerate in trifles, he speaks no harsh words, he and his bride go about together, walk together, read together, and perhaps, if they are very advanced, even work together. But after a few months, or maybe a few years of marriage they seem to have drifted apart, and he finds her often cold and incomprehensible. Few men will acknowledge this even to their best friends. But each heart knows its own pain.

He may at times laugh, and in the friendliest spirit tease his wife about her contrariness. That is taken by everyone to mean nothing but a playful concealment of his profound love. Probably it is. But gnawing at the very roots of his love is a hateful little worm—the sense that she *is contrary*. He feels that she is at times inexplicably cold; that, sometimes, when he has 'done nothing' she will have tears in her eyes, irrational tears which she cannot explain.

He observes that one week his tender love-making and romantic advances win her to smiles and joyous yielding, and then perhaps a few days later the same, or more impassioned, tenderness on his part is met by coldness or a forced appearance of warmth, which, while he may make no comment upon it, hurts him acutely. And this deep, inexplicable hurt is often the beginning of the end of his love. Men like to feel that they understand their dearest one, and that she is a rational being.

After inexplicable misunderstanding has continued for some time, if the man is of at all a jealous nature he will search his wife's acquaintances for someone whom she may have met, for someone who may momentarily have diverted her attention. For however hard it is for the natural man to believe that anyone could step into *his* shoes, some are ready to seek the explanation of their own ill success in a rival. On some occasion when her coldness puzzles him the man is perhaps conscious that his love, his own desires, are as ardent as they were a few days before; then, knowing so intimately his own heart, he is sure of the steadiness of its love, and he feels acutely the romantic passion to which her beauty stirs him; he remembers perhaps that a few days earlier his ardour had awakened a response in her; therefore, he reaches what appears to him to be the infallible logical deduction—that either there must be some rival or his bride's nature is incomprehensible, contrary, capricious. Both thoughts to madden.

With capriciousness, man in general has little patience. Caprice renders his best efforts null and void. Woman's caprice is, or appears to be, a negation of reason. And as reason is man's most precious and hard-won faculty, the one which has raised mankind from the ranks of the brute creation, he cannot bear to see it apparently flouted.

That his bride should lack logic and sweet reasonableness is a flaw it hurts him to recognise in her. He has to crush the thought down.

It may then happen that the young man, himself pained and bewildered at having pained his bride by the very ardour of his affection, may strive to please her by placing restraint upon himself. He may ask himself: Do not religious and many kinds of moral teachers preach restraint to the man? He reads the books written for the guidance of youth, and finds 'restraint,' 'self-control,' in general terms (and often irrationally) urged in them all. His next step may then be to curtail the expression of his tender feelings, and to work hard and late in the evenings instead of kissing his bride's fingers and coming to her for sweet communion in the dusk.

And then, if he is at all observant, he may be aggrieved and astonished to find her again wistful or hurt. With the tender longing to *understand*, which is so profound a characteristic in all the best of our young men, he begs, implores, or pets her into telling him some part of the reason for her fresh grievance. He discovers to his amazement that *this* time she is hurt because he had not made those very advances which so recently had repelled her, and had been with such difficulty repressed by his intellectual efforts.

He asks himself in despair: What is a man to do? If he is 'educated,' he probably devours all the books on sex he can obtain. But in them he is not likely to find much real guidance. He learns from them that 'restraint' is advised from every point of view, but according to the character of the author he will find that 'restraint' means having the marriage relations with his wife not more than three times a week, or once a month—or never at all except for the procreation of children. He finds no *rational* guidance based on natural law.

According to his temperament then, he may begin to practise 'restraint.'

But it may happen, and indeed it has probably happened in every marriage once or many times, that the night comes when the man who has heroically practised restraint, accidentally discovers his wife in tears on her solitary pillow.

He seeks for advice indirectly from his friends, perhaps from his doctor. But can his local doctor or his friends tell him more than the chief European authorities on this subject? The famous Professor Forel ('The Sexual Question,' transl. 1908) gives the following advice:—

The reformer, Luther, who was a practical man, laid down the average rule of two or three connections a week in marriage, at the time of highest sexual power. I may say that my numerous observations as a physician have generally confirmed this rule, which seems to me to conform very well to the normal state to which *man*[1] has become gradually adapted during thousands of years.

[1] The italics are mine.—M.C.S.

This pronouncement of an exceptionally advanced and broad-minded thinker serves to show how little attention has hitherto been paid to the woman's side of this question, or to ascertaining *her* natural requirements.

Husbands who would consider this average as an imprescriptable right would, however, make wrong pretensions, for it is quite possible for a normal man to contain himself much longer, and it is his duty to do so, not only when his wife is ill, but also during menstruation and pregnancy.

Many men will not be so considerate as to follow this advice, which represents a high standard of living; but, on the other hand, there are many who are willing to go not only so far, but further than this in their self-suppression in order to attain their heart's desire, the happiness of their mate, and consequently their own life's joy.

However willing they may be to go further, the great question for the man is: Where?

There are innumerable leaders anxious to lead in many different directions. The young husband may try first one and then the other, and still find his wife unsatisfied, incomprehensible— capricious. Then it may be that, disheartened, he tires, and she sinks into the dull apathy of acquiescence in her 'wifely duty.' He is left with an echo of resentment in his heart. If only she had not been so capricious, they would still have been happy, he fancies.

Many writers, novelists, poets and dramatists have represented the uttermost tragedy of human life as due to the incomprehensible contrariness of the feminine nature. The kindly ones smile, perhaps a little patronisingly, and tell us that women are more instinctive, more child-like, less reasonable than men. The bitter ones sneer or reproach or laugh at this in women they do not understand, and which, baffling *their* intellect, appears to them to be irrational folly.

It seems strange that those who search for natural law in every province of our universe should have neglected the most vital subject, the one which concerns us all infinitely more than the naming of planets or the collecting of insects. Women is *not* essentially capricious; some of the laws of her being might have been discovered long ago had the existence of law been suspected. But it has suited the general structure of society much better for men to shrug their shoulders and smile at women as irrational and capricious creatures, to be courted when it suited them, not to be studied.

Vaguely, perhaps, men have realised that much of the charm of life lies in the *sex-differences* between men and women; so they have snatched at the easy theory that women differ from themselves by being capricious. Moreover, by attributing to mere caprice the coldness which at times comes over the most ardent woman, man was unconsciously justifying himself for at any time coercing her to suit himself.

Circumstances have so contrived that hitherto the explorers and scientific investigators, the historians and statisticians, the poets and artists have been mainly men. Consequently woman's side of the joint life has found little or no expression. Woman has been content to mould herself to the shape desired by man wherever possible, and she has stifled her natural feelings and her own deep thoughts as they welled up.

Most women have never realised intellectually, but many have been dimly half-conscious, that woman's nature is set to rhythms over which man has no more control than he has over the tides of the sea. While the ocean can subdue and dominate man and laugh at his attempted restrictions, woman has bowed to man's desire over her body, and, regardless of its pulses, he approaches her or not as is his will. Some of her rhythms defy him—the moon-month tide of menstruation, the cycle of ten moon-months of bearing the growing child and its birth at the end of the tenth wave—these are essentials too strong to be mastered by man. But the subtler ebb and flow of woman's sex has escaped man's observation or his care.

If a swimmer comes to a sandy beach when the tide is out and the waves have receded, leaving sand where he had expected deep water—does he, baulked of his bathe, angrily call the sea 'capricious'?

But the tenderest bridegroom finds only caprice in his bride's coldness when she yields her sacrificial body while her sex-tide is at the ebb.

There is another side to this problem, one perhaps even less considered by society. There is the tragic figure of the loving woman whose love-tide is at the highest, and whose husband does not recognise the delicate signs of her ardour. In our anaemic, artificial days it often happens that the man's desire is a surface need, quickly satisfied, colourless, and lacking beauty, and that he has no knowledge of the rich complexities of love-making which an initiate of love's mysteries enjoys. To such a man his wife may indeed seem petulant, capricious, or resentful without reason.

Welling up in her are the wonderful tides, scented and enriched by the myriad experiences of the human race from its ancient days of leisure and flower-wreathed love-making, urging her to transports and to self-expressions, were the man but ready to take the first step in the initiative or to recognise and welcome it in her. Seldom dare any woman, still more seldom dare a wife, risk the blow at her heart which would be given were she to offer charming love-play to which the man did not respond. To the initiate she will be able to reveal that the tide is up by a hundred subtle signs, upon which he will seize with delight. But if her husband is blind to them there is for her nothing but silence, self-suppression, and their inevitable sequence of self-scorn, followed by resentment towards the man who places her in such a position of humiliation while talking of his 'love.'

So unaware of the elements of the physiological reactions of women are many modern men that the case of Mrs G. is not exceptional. Her husband was accustomed to pet her and have relations with her frequently, but yet he never took any trouble to rouse in her the necessary preliminary feeling for mutual union. She had married as a very ignorant girl, but often vaguely felt a sense of something lacking in her husband's love. Her husband had never kissed her except on the lips and cheek, but once at the crest of the wave of her sex-tide (all unconscious that it was so) she felt a yearning to feel his head, his lips, pressed against her bosom. The sensitive inter-relation between a woman's breasts and the rest of her sex-life is not only a bodily thrill, but there is a world of poetic beauty in the longing of a loving woman for the unconceived child which melts in mists of tenderness toward her lover, the soft touch of whose lips can thus rouse her mingled joy. Because she shyly asked him, Mrs G.'s husband gave her one swift unrepeated kiss upon her bosom. He was so ignorant that he did not know that her husband's lips upon her breast melt a wife to tenderness and are one of a husband's first and surest ways to make her physically ready for complete union. In this way he inhibited her natural desire, and as he never did anything to stir it, she never had any physical pleasure in their relation. Such prudish or careless husbands, content with their own satisfaction, little know the pent-up aching, or even resentment, which may eat into a wife's heart, and ultimately may affect her whole health.

Often the man is also the victim of the purblind social customs which make sex-knowledge *tabu*.

It has become a tradition of our social life that the ignorance of woman about her own body and that of her future husband is a flower-like innocence. And to such an extreme is this sometimes pushed, that not seldom is a girl married unaware that married life will bring her into physical relations with her husband fundamentally different from those with her brother. When she discovers the true nature of his body, and learns the part she has to play as a wife, she may refuse utterly to agree to her husband's wishes. I know one pair of which the husband, chivalrous and loving, had to wait years before his bride recovered from the shock of the discovery of the meaning of marriage and was able to allow him a natural relation. There have been not a few brides whom the horror of the first night of marriage with a man less considerate has driven to suicide or insanity.

That girls can reach a marriageable age without some knowledge of the realities of marriage would seem incredible were it not a fact. One highly-educated lady intimately known to me told me that when she was about eighteen she suffered many months of agonising apprehension that she was about to have a baby because a man had snatched a kiss from her lips at a dance.

When girls so brought up are married it is a *rape* for the husband to insist on his 'marital rights' at once. It will be difficult or impossible for such a bride ever after to experience the joys of sex-union, for such a beginning must imprint upon her consciousness the view that the man's animal nature dominates him.

In a magazine I came across a poem which vividly expresses this peculiarly feminine sorrow:

> . . . To mate with men who have no soul above
> Earth grubbing; who, the bridal night, forsooth,
> Killed sparks that rise from instinct fires of life,
> And left us frozen things, alone to fashion
> Our souls to dust, masked with the name of wife—
> Long years of youth—love years—the years of passion
> Yawning before us. So, shamming to the end,
> All shrivelled by the side of him we wed,
> Hoping that peace may riper years attend,
> Mere odalisques are we—well housed, well fed.

KATHERINE NELSON.*

Many men who enter marriage sincerely and tenderly may yet have some previous experience of bought 'love.' It is then not unlikely that they may fall into the error of explaining their wife's experiences in terms of the reactions of the prostitute. They argue that, because the prostitute showed physical excitement and pleasure in union, if the bride or wife does not do so, then she is 'cold' or 'undersexed'. They may not realise that often all the bodily movements which the prostitute makes are studied and simulated because her client enjoys his climax best when the woman in his arms simultaneously thrills.

As Forel says ('The Sexual Question,' 1908, Engl. trans.): 'The company of prostitutes often renders men incapable of understanding feminine psychology, for prostitutes are hardly more than automata trained for the use of male sensuality. When men look among these for the sexual psychology of woman they find only their own mirror.'

Fate is often cruel to men, too. More high-spirited young men than the world imagines strive for and keep their purity to give their brides; if such a man then marries a woman who is soiled, or, on the other hand, one who is so 'pure' and prudish that she denies him union with her body, his noble achievement seems bitterly vain. On the other hand, it may be that after years of fighting with his hot young blood a man has given up and gone now and again for relief to prostitutes, and then later in life has met the woman who is his mate, and whom, after remorse for his soiled past, and after winning her forgiveness for it, he marries. Then, unwittingly, he may make the wife suffer either by interpreting her in the light of the other women or perhaps (though this happens less frequently) by setting her absolutely apart from them. I know of a man who, after a loose life, met a woman whom he reverenced and adored. He married her, but to preserve her 'purity,' her difference from the others, he never consummated his marriage with her. She was strangely unhappy, for she loved him passionately and longed for children. She appeared to him to be pining 'capriciously' when she became thin and neurotic.

Perhaps this man might have seen his own behaviour in a truer light had he known that some creatures simply *die* if unmated (see p. 108 Appendix).

The idea that woman is lowered by sex intercourse is very deeply rooted in our present society. Many sources have contributed to this mistaken idea, not the least powerful being the ascetic ideal of the early Church and the fact that man has *used* woman as his instrument so often regardless of her wishes. Women's education, therefore, and the trend of social feeling, has largely been in the direction of freeing her from this and thus mistakenly encouraging the idea that sex-life is a low, physical, and degrading necessity which a pure woman is above enjoying.

In marriage the husband has used his 'marital right'[1] of intercourse when *he* wished it. Both law and custom have strengthened the view that he has the right to approach his wife whenever

---

[1] 'Conjugal Rights.' Notes and Queries. May 16, 1891, p. 383. 'S. writes from the Probate Registry, Somerset House: "Previous to 1733 legal proceedings were recorded in Latin and the word then used where we now speak of *rights* was *obsequies*. For some time after the substitution of English for Latin the term *rites* was usually, if not invariably adopted; *rights* would appear to be a comparatively modern error." '
'Mr. T. E. Paget writes* ("Romeo and Juliet," Act V., Scene III.):

> 'What cursed foot wanders this way to-night
> To cross my obsequies, and true lovers rite?'

'Well may Lord Esher say he has never been able to make out what the phrase "conjugal rights" means. The origin of the term is now clear, and a blunder, which was first made, perhaps, by a type-setter in the early part of the last century, and never exposed until now, has led to a vast amount of misapprehension. Here, too, is another proof that Shakespeare was exceedingly familiar with "legal language." '

he wishes, and that she has no wishes and no fundamental needs in the matter at all.

That woman has a rhythmic sex-tide which, if its indications were obeyed, would ensure not only her enjoyment, but would explode the myth of her capriciousness, seems not to be suspected. We have studied the wave-lengths of water, of sound, of light; but when will the sons and daughters of men study the sex-tide in woman and learn the laws of her Periodicity of Recurrence of desire?

CHAPTER IV

THE FUNDAMENTAL PULSE*

> The judgments of men concerning women are very rarely mat-
> ters of cold scientific observation, but are coloured both by their
> own sexual emotions and by their own moral attitude toward the
> sexual impulse. . . . [Men's] Statements about the sexual
> impulses of women often tell us less about women than about the
> persons who make them.—H. ELLIS*

By the majority of 'nice' people woman is supposed to have no
spontaneous sex impulses. By this I do not mean a sentimental
'falling in love,' but a physical, a physiological state of stimulation
which arises spontaneously and quite apart from any particular
man. It is in truth the *creative* impulse, and is an expression of a
high power of vitality. So widespread in our country is the view
that it is only depraved women who have such feelings (especially
before marriage) that most women would rather die than own
that they *do* at times feel a physical yearning indescribable, but as
profound as hunger for food. Yet many, many women have shown
me the truth of their natures when I have simply and naturally
assumed that of course they feel it—being normal women—and
have asked them only: *When?* From their replies I have collected
facts which are sufficient to overturn many ready-made theories
about women.

Some of the ridiculous absurdities which go by the name of
science may be illustrated by the statement made by Windscheid*
in the Centralblatt für Gynäkologie: 'In the normal woman, especially of the higher social classes, the sexual instinct is acquired,
not inborn; when it is inborn, or awakens by itself, there is
abnormality. Since women do not know this instinct before marriage, they do not miss it when they have no occasion in life to
learn it.' (Ellis transl.)

The negation of this view is expressed in the fable of Hera
quoted by Ellen Key.* Hera sent Iris to earth to seek out three
virtuous and perfectly chaste maidens who were unsoiled by any

dreams of love. Iris found them, but could not take them back to Olympus, for they had already been sent for to replace the superannuated Furies in the infernal regions.

Nevertheless it is true that the whole education of girls, which so largely consists in the concealment of the essential facts of life from them; and the positive teaching so prevalent that the racial instincts are low and shameful; and also the social condition which places so many women in the position of depending on their husband's will not only for the luxuries but for the necessaries of life, have all tended to inhibit natural sex-impulses in women, and to conceal and distort what remains.

It is also true that in our northern climate women are on the whole naturally less persistently stirred than southerners; and it is further true that with the delaying of maturity, due to our ever-lengthening youth, it often happens that a woman is approaching or even past thirty years before she is awake to the existence of the profoundest calls of her nature. For many years before that, however, the unrealised influence, diffused throughout her very system, has profoundly affected her. It is also true that (partly due to the inhibiting influences of our customs, traditions and social code) women may marry before it wakes, and may remain long after marriage entirely unconscious that it surges subdued within them. For innumerable women, too, the husband's regular habits of intercourse, claiming her both when she would naturally enjoy union and when it is to some degree repugnant to her, have tended to flatten out the billowing curves of the line of her natural desire. One result, apparently little suspected, of using the woman as a passive instrument for man's need has been, in effect, to make her that and nothing more. Those men—and there are many—who complain of the lack of ardour in good wives, are often themselves entirely the cause of it. When a woman is claimed at times when she takes no *natural* pleasure in union, it reduces her vitality, and tends to kill her power of enjoying it when the love season returns.

It is certainly true of women as they have been made by the inhibitions of modern conditions, that most of them are only fully awake to the existence of sex after marriage. As we are human beings, the social, intellectual, spiritual side of the love-choice have tended to mask the basic physiological aspect of women's sex-life. To find a woman in whom the currents are not all so entangled that the whole is inseparable into factors, is not easy, but I have found that wives (particularly happy wives whose feelings are not complicated by the stimulus of another love) who have been separated from their husbands for some months through professional or business duties—whose husbands, for instance, are abroad—are the women from whom the best and most definitive evidence of a fundamental rhythm of feeling can be obtained. Such women, yearning daily for the tender comrade-ship and nearness of their husbands, find, in addition, at particular times, an accession of longing for the close physical union of the final sex-act. Many such separated wives feel this; and those I have asked to keep notes of the dates, have, with remarkable unanimity, told me that these times came specially just before and some week or so after the close of menstruation, coming, that is, about every fortnight. It is from such women that I got the first clue to the knowledge of what I call the Law of Periodicity of Recurrence of desire in women.

This law it is possible to represent graphically as a curved line; a succession of crests and hollows as in all wave-lines. Its simplest and most fundamental expression, however, is generally immensely complicated by other stimulations which may bring into it diverse series of waves, or irregular wave-crests. We have all, at some time, watched the regular ripples of the sea breaking against a sand-bank, and noticed that the influx of another current of water may send a second system of waves at right angles to the first, cutting athwart them, so that the two series of waves pass through each other.

Woman is so sensitive and responsive an instrument, and so liable in our modern civilised world to be influenced by innumerable sets of stimuli, that it is perhaps scarcely surprising that the deep, underlying waves of her primitive sex-tides have been obscured, and entangled so that their regular sequence has been masked in the choppy turmoil of her sea, and their existence has been largely unsuspected, and apparently quite unstudied.

For some years I have been making as scientific and detailed a study as possible of this extremely complex problem. Owing to the frank and scientific attitude of a number of women, and the ready and intimate confidence of many more, I have obtained a number of most interesting facts from which I think it is already possible to deduce a generalisation which is illuminating, and may be of great medical and sociological value. A detailed statement of this will be given in a scientific publication, but as it bears very intimately on the subject of the present chapter, a short and simple account of my conclusions must be given here.

It is first necessary to consider several other features of woman's life, however.

The obvious moon-month rhythm in woman, so obvious that it *cannot* be overlooked, has been partially studied in its relation to some of the ordinary functions of her life. Experiments have been made to show its influence on the rate of breathing, the muscular strength, the temperature, the keenness of sight, etc., and these results have even been brought together and pictured in a single curved diagram supposed to show the variability in woman's capacities at the different times in her twenty-eight-day cycle.

But it brings home to one how little original work even in this field has yet been done, that the same identical diagram is repeated from book to book, and in Marshall's Physiology it is 'taken from Sellheim,' in Havelock Ellis 'from Von Ott,' and in other books is re-copied and attributed to still other sources, but it is always the same old diagram.

This diagram is reproduced by one learned authority after another, yet nearly every point on which this curve is based appears to have been disputed.

According to this curve, woman's vitality rises during the few days before menstruation, sinks to its lowest ebb during menstruation and rises shortly after, and then runs nearly level till it begins to rise again before the next menstrual period. This simple curve may or may not be true for woman's temperature, muscular strength, and the other relatively simple things which have been investigated. My work and observations on a large number of women all go to show that this curve does *not* represent the waves of woman's sex-vitality.

The whole subject is so complex and so little studied that it is difficult to enter upon it at all without going into many details which may seem remote or dull to the general reader. Even a question which we must all have asked, and over which we have probably pondered in vain—namely, what is menstruation?— cannot yet be answered. To the lay mind it would seem that this question should be answerable at once by any doctor; but many medical men are still far from being able to reply to it even approximately correctly. (See also Appendix, note 2.)

There are a good many slight variations among us, ranging from a three to a five weeks 'month,' but the majority of the women of our race have a moon-month of twenty-eight days, once during which comes the flow of menstruation. If we draw out a chart with succeeding periods of twenty-eight days each, looking on each period as a unit: When in this period is it that a normal healthy woman feels desire or any upwelling of her sex-tides?

The few statements which are made in general medical and physiological literature on the subject of sex feeling in women are generally very guarded and vague. Marshall ('Physiology of Reproduction,' p. 138), for instance, says: 'The period of most acute sexual feeling is generally just after the close of the menstrual period.' Ellis speaks of desire being stronger before and sometimes also after menstruation, and appears to lean to the view that it is natural for desire to coincide with the menstrual flow.

After the most careful inquiries I have come to the conclusion that the general confusion regarding this subject is due partly to the great amount of variation which exists between different individuals, and partly to the fact that very few women have any idea of taking any scientific interest in life, and partly to the fact that the more profound, fundamental rhythm of sex desire which I have come to the conclusion exists or is potential in every normal woman, is covered over or masked by the more superficial and temporary influences due to a great variety of stimuli or inhibitions in modern life. For the present consideration I have tried to disentangle the profound and natural rhythm from the more irregular surface waves.

The chart given opposite may assist in making graphically clear what has been said in these last few pages. It is compounded from a number of individual records, and shows a fair average chart of the rhythmic sequence of superabundance and flagging in woman's sex-vitality. The tops of the wave-crests come with remarkable regularity, so that there are two wave-crests in each twenty-eight-day month. The one comes on the two or three days just *before* menstruation, the other after; but after menstruation has ceased there is a nearly level interval, bringing the next wave-crest to the two or three days which come about eight or nine days after the close of menstruation—that is, just around the fourteen days, or half the moon month, since the last wave-crest. If this is put in its simplest way, one may say that there are fortnightly periods of desire, arranged so that one period comes always just *before* each menstrual flow. According to her vitality at the time, and the general health of the woman, the length of each desire-period, or, as we might say, the size and complexity of each wave-crest, depends. Sometimes for the whole of as much as, or even more than three days, she may be ardently and quite naturally stimulated, while at another time the same woman, if she is tired and over-worked, may be conscious of desire for only a few hours, or even less.

The effects of fatigue, city life, bad feeding, and, indeed, of most outward circumstances may be very marked, and may for years, or all her life, so reduce her vitality that a woman may never have experienced any spontaneous sex-impulse at all.

The effects of fatigue, which reduces the vital energy, even in a normal, strongly sexed woman, can be seen in the second curve (p. 44), where at *a* the intermediate wave-crest is very much reduced. This is not a generalised chart, but a detailed record of an actual individual case.

Curves similar to those shown on page 43 represent in general terms a simplified view of what my research leads me to believe to be the normal, spontaneous sex-tide in women of our

CHART I

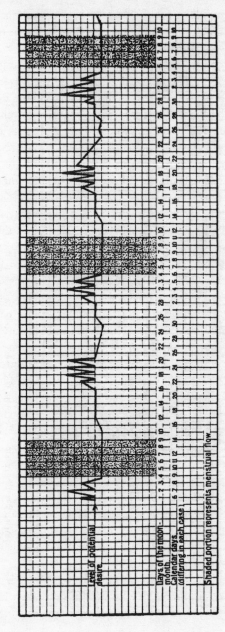

Curve showing the Periodicity of Recurrence of natural desire in healthy women. Various causes make slight irregularities in the position, size and duration of the 'wave-crests,' but the general rhythmic sequence is apparent.

CHART II

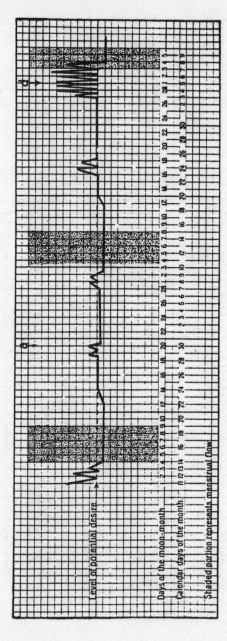

Curve showing the depressing effects on the 'wave-crests' of fatigue and over-work. Crest *a* represented only by a feeble and transient up-welling. Shortly before and during the time of the crest *d* Alpine air restored the vitality of the subject. The increased vitality is shown by the height and number of the apices of this wave-crest.

race. As one young married woman confided to me, her longing for bodily union with her husband, as distinct from her longing for his daily companionship, seemed to well up naturally 'like clockwork,' and this when he had been long away from her. But human beings vary remarkably in every particular, and just as no two people have the same features, so no two people would have *absolutely* identical curves were they recorded in sufficient detail. Many a woman is particularly conscious of only one period in each moon-month. Of such women, some feel the period which comes before menstruation, and some feel the one which follows it. In those who generally feel only one, the second period is sometimes felt when they are particularly well, or only when they read exciting novels, or meet the man they love at a time coinciding with the natural, but suppressed, time of desire. There are a few women, who seem to be really a little abnormal, who feel the strongest desire actually during the menstrual flow.

If anyone who reads this thinks to test my view by questioning a number of women, the result will probably appear very conflicting, partly because it is not often that women will tell the truth about such a thing, and partly because in the larger number of women either one or the other period is the more acute and is the one they observe in themselves—if they have observed anything. But a delicate and more accurate investigation of such cases will often bring to light the existence of the second crest of vitality. Once the fundamental idea is grasped, much that appeared obscure or of no significance becomes plain and full of meaning. One lady doctor with whom I discussed my view at once said that it illuminated many observations she had made on her patients, but had not brought together or explained.

There is but little evidence to be found in scientific works on sex, but an interesting instance is mentioned by Forel ('The Sexual Question,' Engl. Transl. page 92) in another connection. He says: 'A married woman confessed to me, when I reproached her for being unfaithful to her husband, that she desired coitus at least once a fortnight, and that when her husband was not there she took the first comer.' Forel did not see any law in this. We may perhaps all see in her want of self-control a grievous *moral* abnormality, but in her fortnightly periods of desire she fits perfectly into the physiological law which, it appears to me, governs the normal sex-tides of our race.

In this connection it is of interest to note the decrees of the Mosaic Law regarding marriage intercourse. Not only was all intercourse with a woman during her menstruation period very heavily punished (see Leviticus xx. 18: 'If a man lie with a woman having her sickness . . . both of them shall be cut off from among their people'), but the Mosaic Law provided that women should be protected from intercourse for some days *after* each such period. The results obtained by my independent investigation thus find some support in this ancient wisdom of the East. Modern writers are inclined to deride the Mosaic Law on the ground that it prohibits intercourse just at the time when *they think* sex feeling should be strongest. But it does not appear on what grounds they make the latter statement, nor do they give any scientific data in support of it. Thus Galabin* in his Manual of Midwifery says: 'In the Jewish law women are directed to abstain[1] from coitus during menstruation and for seven days after its cessation. Strict observers of the law are said to go beyond what is commanded in Leviticus, and even if discharge lasts only for an hour or two, to observe five days during which the discharge might last, for the period itself, and add to these seven clear days, making twelve in all. It is much to be doubted whether a whole nation was ever induced to practise abstinence at the period of most acute sexual feeling.' But, as will readily be recognised, the old Jewish plan of having twelve clear days after the beginning of menstruation before the next union is in almost exact harmony with the Law of Periodicity of Recurrence of women's desire shown in my charts, pp. 43, 44.

These comparatively simple curves represent what I would postulate as the normal spontaneous up-welling of natural desire in woman. These are the foundations on which the edifice of the physical expression of love may be built. It must not be forgotten, however, that, particularly in modern luxurious life, there are

---

[1] NOTE.—In Leviticus xv. it is the *man* who is directed to abstain from touching the woman at this period, and who is rendered unclean if he does.—M.C.S.

innumerable excitements which may *stimulate* sexual feeling, just as there are many factors in our life which tend to inhibit or retard it. A woman may be, like a man, so swayed by a great love that there is not a day in the whole month when her lover's touch, his voice, the memory of his smile, does not stir her into the thrilling longing for the uttermost union. Hence it is often difficult, particularly for a woman dwelling with the man she loves, to recognise this rhythm in herself, for she may be perpetually stimulated by her love and by his being.

I am convinced, however, that ordinarily, whether she recognises it by outward signs or not, a fortnightly rhythm profoundly influences the average woman, and hence that it fundamentally affects the marriage relation in every way. The burning magnificence of an overpowering lifelong love is not given to many, and a husband who desires lasting and mutual happiness in his marriage will carefully study his wife, observe how far she has a normal rhythm, and in what she has little personal traits. He will then endeavour to adapt his demands on her so that they are in harmony with her nature.

This mutual adaptation is not an entirely simple matter, and will be considered in the next chapter.

CHAPTER V

MUTUAL ADJUSTMENT

'Love worketh no ill to his neighbour.'—St Paul.

In the average man of our race desire knows no season beyond the slight slackening of the winter months and the heightening of spring. Some men have observed in themselves a faintly-marked monthly rhythm; but in the majority of men desire, even if held in stern check, is merely slumbering. It is always present, ever ready to wake at the lightest call, and often so spontaneously insistent as to require perpetual conscious repression.

It would go ill with the men of our race had women retained the wild animals' infrequent seasonal rhythm, and with it her inviolable rights in her own body save at the mating season. Woman, too, has acquired a much more frequent rhythm; but, as it does not equal man's, he has tended to ignore and over-ride it, coercing her at all times and seasons, either by force, or by the even more compelling power of 'divine' authority and social tradition.

If man's desire is perpetual and woman's intermittent; if man's desire naturally wells up every day or every few days, and woman's only every fortnight or every month, it may appear at first sight impossible for the unwarped needs of both natures simultaneously to be satisfied.

The sense that a satisfactory mutual adjustment is not within the realms of possibility has, indeed, obsessed our race for centuries. The result has been that the supposed need of one of the partners has tended to become paramount, and we have established the social traditions of a husband's 'rights' and wifely 'duty'. As one man quite frankly said to me: 'As things are it is impossible for both sexes to get what they want. One *must* be sacrificed. And it is better for society that it should be the woman.'

Nevertheless, the men who consciously sacrifice the women are in a minority. Most men act in ignorance. Our code, however, has blindly sacrificed not only the woman, but with her the happiness of the majority of men, who, in total ignorance of its meaning and results, have grown up thinking that women should submit to regularly frequent, or even nightly, intercourse. For the sake of a few moments of physical pleasure they lose realms of ever-expanding joy and tenderness; and while men and women may not realise the existence of an untrodden paradise, they both suffer, if only half consciously, from being shut out from it.

Before making some suggestions which may help married people to find not only a *via media* of mutual endurance, but a *via perfecta* of mutual joy, it is necessary to consider a few points about the actual nature of man's 'desire.' In the innumerable books addressed to the young which I have read, I have not found one which gives certain points regarding the meaning of the male sex-phenomena which must be grasped before it is possible to give rational guidance to intelligent young men. The general ground plan of our physiology is told to us in youth because it so obviously is right for us to know it accurately and in a clean scientific way, rather than to be perpetually perplexed by fantastic imaginings. But the physiology of our most profoundly disturbing functions is ignored—in my opinion, criminally ignored. To describe the essentials, simple, direct and scientific language is necessary, though it may surprise those who are accustomed only to the hazy vagueness which has led to so much misapprehension of the truth. Every mating man and woman should know the following: The sex organs of a man consist not only of the tissues which give rise to the living, moving, ciliated cells, the *sperms*, and of the penis through which they pass and by means of which they are directed into the proper place for their deposition, the woman's vagina. Associated with these primary and essential structures there are other tissues and glands which have numerous subsidiary but yet very important parts to play; some of which influence almost every organ in the body. Man's penis, when unstimulated, is soft, small and drooping. But when stimulated, either by physical touch which acts through the nerves and muscles directly, or indirectly through messages from the brain, it increases greatly in size, and becomes stiff, turgid and erect. Many men imagine that the turgid condition of an erection is due to the local accumulation of sperms, and that these can only be naturally got rid of by an ejaculation. This is entirely wrong. The enlargement of the penis is not at all due to the presence of actual sperm, but is due to the effects of the nervous reaction on the blood-vessels, leading to the filling, principally of the *veins*, and much less of the arteries. As the blood enters but does not leave the penis, the venous cavities in it fill up with venous blood until the whole is rigid. When rigid this organ is able to penetrate the female entrance, and there the further stimulation calls out the sperms from their storehouses, the seminal vesicles in the testes, and they pass down the channel (the urethra) and are expelled. If this is clear, it will be realised that the stiffening and erection does not *necessarily* call for relief in the ejaculation of sperm. If the veins can empty themselves, as they naturally do when the nervous excitement which restricted them locally passes, the erection will subside without any loss of sperms, by the mere passing back of the locally excessive blood into the ordinary circulatory system. This can happen quite naturally and healthily when the nerves are soothed, either physically or as a result of a sense of mental peace and exaltation. When, on the other hand, the local excitement culminates in the calling up and expulsion of the sperms, after it has once started the ejaculation becomes quite involuntary and the sperms and the secretions associated with them pass out of the system and are entirely lost.

Of what does this loss consist? It is estimated that there are somewhere between two and five hundred million sperms in a single average ejaculation.[1] Each single one of these (in healthy men) is capable of fertilising a woman's egg-cell and giving rise to a new human being. (Thus by a single ejaculation one man might fertilise nearly all the marriageable women in the world!) Each single one of those minute sperms carries countless hereditary traits, and each consists very largely of nuclear plasm—the most highly-specialised and richest substance in our bodies. It is not

[1] See Pflügers Archiv., 1891.

surprising, therefore, to find that the analysis of the chemical nature of the ejaculated fluid reveals among other things a remarkably high percentage of calcium and phosphoric acid— both precious substances in our organisation.

It is therefore the greatest mistake to imagine that the semen is something to be got rid of *frequently*—all the vital energy and the precious chemical substances which go to its composition can be better utilised by being transformed into other creative work on most days of the month. And so mystic and wonderful are the chemical transformations going on in our bodies that the brain can often set this alchemy in motion, particularly if the brain is helped by *knowledge*. A strong will can often calm the nerves which regulate the blood supply, and order the distended veins of the penis to retract and subside without wasting the semen in an ejaculation.

But while it is good that a man should be able to do this often, it is not good to try to do it always. The very restraint which adds to a man's strength up to a point, taxes his strength when carried beyond it. It is my belief that just sufficient restraint to carry him through the ebb-tides of his wife's sex-rhythm is usually the right amount to give the best strength, vigour, and joy to a man if both are normal people. If the wife has, as I think the majority of healthy, well-fed young women will be found to have, a fort-nightly consciousness or unconscious *potentiality* of desire, then the two should find a perfect mutual adjustment in having fort-nightly unions; for this need not be confined to only a single union on such occasion. Many men, who can well practise restraint for twelve or fourteen days, will find that one union only will not then thoroughly satisfy them; and if they have the good fortune to have healthy wives, they will find that the latter, too, have the desire for several unions in the course of a day or two. If the wave-crests on page 43 are studied, it will be seen that they spread over two or three days and show several small minor crests. This is what happens when a woman is thoroughly well and vital; her desire recurs during a day or two, sometimes even every few hours if it does not, and sometimes even when it does, receive satisfaction.

Expressed in general terms (which, of course, will not fit everybody) my view may be formulated thus: The mutually best regulation of intercourse in marriage is to have three or four days of repeated unions, followed by about ten days without any unions at all, unless some strong external stimulus has stirred a mutual desire.

I have been interested to discover that the people known to me who have accidentally fixed upon this arrangement of their lives are *happy*: and it should be noted that it fits in with the charts I give which represent the normal, spontaneous feeling of so many women.

There are many women, however, who do not feel, or who may not at first recognise, a second, but have only one time of natural pleasure in sex in each moon-month. Many men of strong will and temperate lives will be able so to control themselves that they can adjust themselves to this more retrained sex-life, as do some with whom I am acquainted. On the other hand, there will be many who find this period too long to live through without using a larger amount of energy in restraining their impulse than is justifiable. It seems to me never justifiable to spend so much energy and will power on restraining natural impulses, that valuable work and intellectual power and poise are made to suffer. If, then, a strongly-sexed husband, who finds it a real loss to his powers of work to endure through twenty-six days of abstinence, should find himself married to a wife whose vitality is so low that she can only take pleasure in physical union once in her moon-month (in some it will be before, in some a little time after, her menstrual flow), he should note carefully the time she is spontaneously happy in their union, and then at any cost restrain himself through the days immediately following, and about a fortnight after her time of desire he should set himself ardently to woo her. Unless she is actually out of health he is more likely then than at any other time to succeed not only in winning her compliance, but also in giving her the proper feeling and attaining mutual ecstasy.

The husband who so restrains himself, even if it is hard to do it, will generally find that he is a thousand-fold repaid not only by the increasing health and happiness of his wife, and the much intenser pleasure he gains from their mutual intercourse, but also by his own added vitality and sense of self-command. A fortnight is not too long for a healthy man to restrain himself with advantage.

Sir Thomas Clouston says ('Before I Wed,' 1913, page 84): 'Nature has also so arranged matters that the more constantly control is exercised the more easy and effective it becomes. It becomes a *habit*. The less control is exercised the greater tendency there is for a desire to become a *craving* of an uncontrollable kind, which is itself of the nature of disease, and means death sooner or later.' This conclusion is not only the result of the intellectual and moral experience of our race, but is supported by physiological experiments.

While a knowledge of the fundamental laws of our being should in the main regulate our lives, so complex are we, so sensitive to a myriad impressions, that clock-work regularity can never rule us.

Even where the woman is strongly sexed, with a well-marked recurrence of desire, which is generally satisfied by fortnightly unions, it may not infrequently happen that, in between these periods, there may be additional special occasions when there springs up a mutual longing to unite. These will generally depend on some event in the lovers' lives which stirs their emotions; some memory of past passion, such as an anniversary of their wedding, or perhaps will be due to a novel, poem, or picture which moves them deeply. If the man she loves plays the part of tender wooer, even at times when her passion would not *spontaneously* arise, a woman can generally be stirred so fundamentally as to give a passionate return. But at the times of her ebb-tides the stimulus will have to be stronger than at the high tides, and it will then generally be found that the appeal must be made even more through her emotional and spiritual nature and less through the physical than usual.

The supreme law for husbands is: Remember that each act of union must be tenderly wooed for and won, and that no union should ever take place unless the woman also desires it and is made physically ready for it. (See pages 55–6.)

While in most marriages the husband has to restrain himself to meet the wife's less frequently recurrent rhythm, there are, on the other hand, marriages in which the husband is so under-sexed that he cannot have ordinary union save at very infrequent intervals without a serious effect on his health. If such a man is married to a woman who has inherited an unusually strong and over-frequent desire, he may suffer by union with her, or may cause her suffering by refusing to unite. It is just possible that for such people the method of Karezza* (see Dr A. Stockham's book 'Karezza' on the subject) might bring them both the health and peace they need; conserving the man's vital energy from the loss of which he suffers, and giving the woman the sense of union and physical nerve-soothing she requires. But the variations in the sex-needs and the sex-ideas of different healthy people are immense, far greater than can be suggested in this book.

Ellis states that the Queen of Aragon ordained that six times a day was the proper rule in legitimate marriage! So abnormally sexed a woman would to-day probably succeed in killing by exhaustion a succession of husbands, for the man who could match such a desire is rare, though perhaps less exceptional than such a woman.

Though the timing and the frequency of union are the points about which questions are oftenest asked by the ignorant and well-meaning, and are most misunderstood, yet there are other fundamental facts concerning coitus about which even medical men seem surprisingly ignorant. Regarding these, a simple statement of the physiological facts is essential.

An impersonal and scientific knowledge of the structure of our bodies is the surest safeguard against prurient curiosity and lascivious gloating. This knowledge at the back of the minds of the lovers, though not perhaps remembered as such, may also spare the unintentioned cruelty of handling which so readily injures one whose lover is ignorant.

What actually happens in an act of union should be known. After the preliminaries have mutually roused the pair, the stimulated penis, enlarged and stiffened, is pressed into the woman's vagina. Ordinarily when a woman is not stimulated, the walls of this canal, as well as the exterior lips of soft tissue surrounding it, are dry and rather crinkled, and the vaginal opening is smaller than the man's extended penis. But when the woman is what is physiologically called tumescent (that is, when she is ready for union and has been profoundly stirred) these parts are flushed by the internal blood supply and to some extent are turgid like those of the man, while a secretion of mucous lubricates the channel of the vagina. In an ardent woman the vagina may even spontaneously open and close. (So powerful is the influence of thought on our bodily structure, that in some people all these physical results may be brought about by the thought of the loved one, by the enjoyment of tender words and kisses, and the beautiful subtleties of wooing.) It can therefore be readily imagined that when the man tries to enter a woman whom he has *not* wooed to the point of stimulating her natural physical reactions of preparation, he is endeavouring to force his entry through a dry-walled opening too small for it. He may thus cause the woman actual pain, apart from the mental revolt and loathing she is likely to feel for a man who so regardlessly user her. On the other hand, in the tumescent woman the opening, already naturally expanded, is lubricated by mucous, and all the nerves and muscles are ready to react and easily accept the man's entering organ. This account is of the meeting of two who have been already married. The first union of a virgin girl differs, of course, from all others, for on that occasion the hymen is broken. One would think that every girl who was about to be married would be told of this necessary rupturing of the membrane and the temporary pain it will cause her; but even still large numbers of girls are allowed to marry in complete and cruel ignorance.

It should be realised that a man does not woo and win a woman once for all when he marries her: *he must woo her before every separate act of coitus*, for each act corresponds to a marriage as other creatures know it. Wild animals are not so foolish as man; a wild animal does not unite with his female without the wooing characteristic of his race, whether by stirring her by a display of his strength in fighting another male, or by exhibiting his beautiful feathers or song. And we must not forget that the wild animals are assisted by nature; they generally only woo just at the season when the female is beginning to feel natural desire. But man, who wants his mate all out of season as well as in it, has a double duty to perform, and must himself rouse, charm, and stimulate her to the local readiness which would have been to some extent naturally prepared for him had he waited till her own desire welled up.

To render a woman ready before uniting with her is not only the merest act of humanity to save her pain, but is of value from the man's point of view, for (unless he is one of those relatively few abnormal and diseased variants who delight only in rape) the man gains an immense increase of sensation from the mutuality thus attained, and the health of both the man and the woman is most beneficially affected.

Assuming now that the two are in the closest mental and spiritual, as well as sensory harmony: in what position should the act be consummated? Men and women, looking into each other's eyes, kissing tenderly on the mouth, with their arms round each other, meet face to face. And that position is symbolic of the coming together of the two who meet together gladly.

It seems incredible that to-day educated men should be found who—apparently on theological grounds—refuse to countenance any other position. Yet one wife told me that she was crushed and nearly suffocated by her husband, so that it took her hours to recover after each union, but that 'on principle' he refused to attempt any other position than the one he chose to consider normal. Mutual well-being should be the guide for each pair.

It is perhaps not generally realised how great are the variations of size, shape, and position of all the sex parts of the body in different individuals, yet they differ more even than the size and characters of all the features of the face and hands. It happens, therefore, that the position which suits most people is unsatisfactory for others. Some, for instance, can only benefit by union when both are lying on their sides. Though medically this is generally considered unfavourable or prohibitive for conception, yet I know women who have had several children and whose husbands always used this position. In this matter every couple should find out for themselves which of the many possible positions best suits them *both*.

When the two have met and united, the usual result is that, after a longer or shorter interval, the man's mental and physical stimulation reaches a climax in sensory intoxication and in the ejaculation of semen. Where the two are perfectly adjusted, the woman simultaneously reaches the crisis of nervous and muscular reactions very similar to his. This mutual orgasm is extremely important (see also p. 63), but in many cases the man's climax comes so swiftly that the woman's reactions are not nearly ready, and she is left without it. Though in some instances the woman may have one or more crises before the man achieves his, it is, perhaps, hardly an exaggeration to say that 70 or 80 per cent of our married women (in the middle classes) are deprived of the full orgasm through the excessive speed of the husband's reactions, or through some mal-adjustment of the relative shapes and positions of the organs. So deep-seated, so profound, are woman's complex sex-instincts as well as her organs, that in rousing them the man is rousing her whole body and soul. And this takes time. More time, indeed, than the average, uninstructed husband gives to it. Yet woman has at the surface a small vestigeal organ called the clitoris, which corresponds morphologically to the man's penis, and which, like it, is extremely sensitive to touch-sensations. This little crest, which lies anteriorly between the inner lips round the vagina, enlarges when the woman is really tumescent, and by the stimulation of movement it is intensely roused and transmits this stimulus to every nerve in her body. But even after a woman's dormant sex-feeling is aroused and all the complex reactions of her being have been set in motion, it may even take as much as from ten to twenty minutes of actual physical union to consummate her feeling, while two or three minutes often completes the union for a man who is ignorant of the need to control his reactions so that both may experience the added benefit of a mutual crisis to love.

A number of well-meaning people demand from men absolute 'continence' save for procreation only. They overlook the

innumerable physiological reactions concerned in the act, as well
as the subtle spiritual alchemy of it, and propound the view that
'the opposition to continence, save for procreation only, has but
one argument to put forward, and that is appetite, selfishness.'
(*The Way of God in Marriage*.)*

I maintain, however, that it should be realised that the complete act of union is a triple consummation. It symbolises, and at
the same time actually enhances, the spiritual union; there are a
myriad subtleties of soul-structures which are compounded in
this alchemy. At the same time the act gives the most intense
physical pleasure and benefit which the body can experience, and
it is a *mutual*, not a selfish, pleasure and profit, more calculated
than anything else to draw out an unspeakable tenderness and
understanding in both partakers of this sacrament; while, thirdly,
it is the act which gives rise to a new life by rendering possible the
fusion of one of the innumerable male sperms with the female
egg-cell.

It often happens nowadays that, dreading the expense and the
physical strain of child-bearing for his wife, the husband practises
what is called *coitus interruptus*—that is, he withdraws just before
the ejaculation, but when he is already so stimulated that the
ejaculation has become involuntary. In this way the semen is
spent, but, as it does not enter the wife's body, fertilisation and,
consequently, procreation cannot take place. This practice, while
it may have saved the woman the anguish of bearing unwanted
children, is yet very harmful to her, and is to be deprecated. It
tends to leave the woman in 'mid-air' as it were; to leave her
stimulated and unsatisfied, and therefore it has a very bad effect
on her nerves and general health, particularly if it is done frequently. The woman, too, loses the advantage (and I am convinced that it is difficult to overstate the physiological advantage)
of the partial absorption of the man's secretions, which must take
place through the large tract of internal epithelium with which
they come in contact. If, as physiology has already proved is the
case, the internal absorption of secretions from the sex organs
plays so large a part in determining the health and character of
remote parts of the body, it is extremely likely that the highly

stimulating secretion of man's semen can and does penetrate and affect the woman's whole organism. Actual experiment has shown that iodine placed in the vagina in solution is so quickly absorbed by the epithelial walls that in an hour it has penetrated the system and is even being excreted. It still remains, however, for scientific experiments to be devised which will enable us to study the effects of the absorption of substances from the semen. On the other hand, *coitus interruptus* is not always harmful for the man, for he has the complete sex-act, though a good many men think its effects on them are undesirable, and it may lead to lack of desire or even impotence toward his wife in a man who practises it with her, or, on the other hand, to a too swift fresh desire from the lack of complete resolution of nervous tension. It is certainly bad when its safety from consequences induces him to frequent indulgence, for thus wastefully to scatter what should be *creative power* is to reduce his own vitality and power of work (see also page 50). By those who have a high appreciation of the value of their creative impulse, and who wish to know the mutual pleasure and enhancement of sex-union without wasting it, this method should not be practised.

It should never be forgotten that without the discipline of control there is no lasting delight in erotic feeling. The fullest delight, even in a purely physical sense, can *only* be attained by those who curb and direct their natural impulses.

Dr Saleeby's words are appropriate in this connection (Introduction to Forel's 'Sexual Ethics,' 1908): 'Professor Forel speaks of subduing the sexual instinct. I would rather speak of transmuting it. The direct method of attack is often futile, always necessitous of effect, but it is possible for us to transmute our sex-energy into higher forms in our individual lives, thus justifying the evolutionary and physiological contention that it is the source of the higher activities of man, of moral indignation, and of the "restless energy" which has changed the surface of the earth.'

Forel says ('The Sexual Question,' 1908): 'Before engaging in a lifelong union, a man and woman ought to explain to each other their sexual feelings so as to avoid deception and incompatibility later on.' This would be admirable advice were it possible for a virgin girl to know much about the reactions and effects upon her mind and body of the act of coitus, but she does not. Actually it often takes several years for eager and intelligent couples fully to probe themselves and to discover the extent and meaning of the immensely profound physiological and spiritual results of marriage. Yet it is true that a noble frankness would save much misery when, as happens not infrequently, one or other of the pair marry with the secret determination to have no children.

So various are we all as individuals, so complex all the reactions and inter-actions of sex relations, that no hard-and-fast rule can be laid down. Each couple, after marriage, must study themselves, and the lover and the beloved must do what best serves them both and gives them the highest degree of mutual joy and power. There are, however, some laws which should be inviolable. Their details can be gathered from the preceding pages, and they are summed up in the words: 'Love worketh no ill to the beloved.'

CHAPTER VI

SLEEP

He giveth His Beloved Sleep.*

THE healing magic of sleep is known to all. Sleeplessness is a punishment for so many different violations of nature's laws, that it is perhaps one of the most prevalent of humanity's innumerable sufferings. While most of the aspects of sleep and sleeplessness have received much attention from specialists in human physiology, the relation between sleep and coitus appears to be but little realised. Yet there is an intimate, profound and quite direct relation between the power to sleep, naturally and refreshingly, and the harmonious relief of the whole system in the perfected sex-act.

We see this very clearly in ordinary healthy man. If, for some reason, he has to live unsatisfied for some time after the acute stirring of his longing for physical contact with his wife, he tends in the interval to be wakeful, restless, and his nerves are on edge.

Then, when the propitious hour arrives, and after the love-play, the growing passion expands, until the transports of feeling find their ending in the explosive completion of the act, at once the tension of his whole system relaxes, and his muscles fall into gentle, easy attitudes of languorous content, and in a few moments the man is sleeping like a child.

This excellent and refreshing sleep falls like a soft curtain of oblivion and saves the man's consciousness from the jar and disappointment of an anti-climax. But not only is this sleep a restorative after the strenuous efforts of the transport, it has peculiarly refreshing powers, and many men feel that after such a sleep their whole system seems rejuvenated.

But how fare women in this event? When they too have had complete satisfaction they similarly relax and slumber.

But as things are to-day it is scarcely an exaggeration to say that the majority of wives are left wakeful and nerve-racked to watch with tender motherly brooding, or with bitter and jealous envy, the slumbers of the men who, through ignorance and care-lessness, have neglected to see that they too had the necessary resolution of nervous tension.

Many married women have told me that after they have had relations with their husbands they are restless, either for some hours or for the whole night; and I feel sure that the prevalent failure on the part of many men to effect orgasms for their wives at each congress, must be a very common source of the sleeplessness and nervous diseases of so many married women.

The relation between the completion of the sex act and sleep in woman is well indicated in the case of Mrs A., who is typical of a large class of wives. She married a man with whom she was passionately in love. Neither she nor her husband had ever had connection with anyone else, and, while they were both keen and intelligent people with some knowledge of biology, neither knew anything of the details of human sex union. For several years her husband had unions with her which gave him some satisfaction and left him ready at once to sleep. Neither he nor she knew that women should have an orgasm, and after every union she was left so 'on edge' and sleepless that never less than several hours would elapse before she could sleep at all, and often she remained wakeful the whole night.

After her husband's death her health improved, and in a year or two she entered into a new relation with a man who was aware of women's needs and spent sufficient time and attention to them to ensure a successful completion for her as well as for himself. The result was that she soon became a good sleeper, with the attendant benefits of restored nerves and health.

Sleep is so complex a process, and sleeplessness the resultant of so many different maladjustments, that it is, of course, possible that the woman may sleep well enough, even if she be deprived of the relief and pleasure of perfect union. But in so many married women sleeplessness and a consequent nervous condition are coupled with a lack of the complete sex relation, that one of the first questions a physician *should* put to those of his women patients who are worn and sleepless is: Whether her husband really fulfils his marital duty in their physical relation.

From their published statements, and their admissions to me, it appears that many practising doctors are either almost unaware of the very existence of orgasm in women, or look upon it as a superfluous and accidental phenomenon. Yet to have had a moderate number of orgasms at some time at least is a necessity for the full development of a woman's health and all her powers.

As this book is written for those who are married, I say nothing here about the lives of those who are still unmarried, though, particularly after the age of thirty has been reached, they may be very difficult and need much study and consideration. It is, however, worth noticing how prevalent sleeplessness is among a class of women who have never had any normal sex-life or allowed any relief to their desires. There is little doubt that the complete lack of a normal sex relation is one of the several factors which render many middle-aged unmarried women nervous and sleepless.

Yet for the unmarried woman the lack is not so acute nor so localised as it is for the married woman who is thwarted in the natural completion of her sex-functions after they have been directly stimulated.

The unmarried woman, unless she be in love with some particular man, has no definite stimulus to her sex desires beyond the natural upwelling of the creative force. The married woman, however, is not only diffusely stirred by the presence of the man she loves, but is also acutely locally and physically stimulated by his relation with her. And if she is then left in mid-air, without natural relief to her tension, she is in this respect far worse off than the unmarried woman.

When a wife is left sleepless through the neglect of the mate who slumbers healthily by her side, it is not surprising if she spends the long hours reviewing their mutual position; and the review cannot yield her much pleasure or satisfaction. For deprived of the physical delight of mutual orgasm (though, perhaps, like so many wives, quite unconscious of all it can give), she sees in the sex act an arrangement where pleasure, relief and subsequent sleep, are all on her husband's side, while she is merely the passive instrument of his enjoyment. Nay, more than that: if following every union she has long hours of wakefulness, she then sees clearly the encroachment on her own health in an arrangement in which she is not merely passive, but is actively abused.

Another of the consequences of the incomplete relation is that often, stirred to a point of wakefulness and vivacity by the preliminary sex-stimulation (of the full meaning of which she may be unconscious), a romantic and thoughtful woman is then most able to talk intimately and tenderly—to speak of the things *most* near and sacred to her heart. And she may then be terribly wounded by the inattention of her husband, which, coming so soon after his ardent demonstrations of affection, appears peculiarly callous. It makes him appear to her to be indifferent to the highest side of marriage—the spiritual and romantic intercourse. Thus she may see in the man going off to sleep in the midst of her love-talk, a gross and inattentive brute—and all because she has never shared the climax of his physical tension, and does not know that its natural reaction is sleep.

These thoughts are so depressing even to the tenderest and most loving woman, and so bitter to one who has other causes of complaint, that in their turn they act on the whole system and increase the damage done by the mere sleeplessness.

The older school of physiologists dealt in methods too crude to realise the physiological results of our thoughts, but it is now well known that anger and bitterness have experimentally recognisable physiological effects, and are injurious to the whole system.

It requires little imagination to see that after months or years of such embittered sleeplessness, the woman tends not only to become neurasthenic but also resentful towards her husband. She is probably too ignorant and unobservant of her own physiology to realise the full meaning of what is taking place, but she feels vaguely that he is to blame, and that she is being sacrificed for what, in her still greater ignorance of *his* physiology, seems to her to be his mere pleasure and self-indulgence.

He, with his health maintained by the natural outlet followed by recuperative sleep, is not likely to be ready to look into the gloomy and shadowy land of vague reproach and inexplicable trivial wrongs which are all the expression she gives to her unformulated physical grievance. So he is likely to set down any resentment she may show to 'nerves' or 'captiousness'; and to be first solicitous, and then impatient, towards her apparently irrelevant complaints.

If he is, as many men are, tender and considerate, he may try to remedy matters by restricting to the extreme limit of what is absolutely necessary for him, the number of times they come together. Unconsciously he thus only makes matters worse; for as a general rule, he is quite unaware of his wife's rhythm, and does not arrange to coincide with it in his infrequent tender embraces. As he is now probably sleeping in another room and not daring to come for the nightly talks and tenderness which are so sweet a privilege of marriage, here, as in other ways, his well-meaning but wrongly-conceived efforts at restraint only tend to drive the pair still further apart.

To make plain the reasonableness of my view regarding sleep, it is necessary to mention some of the immensely profound influences which it is now known that sex exerts, even when not stimulated to its specific use.

In those who are deprived of their sex-organs, particularly when young, many of the other features and organs of the body develop abnormally or fail to appear. Castrated boys (eunuchs) when grown up, tend to have little or no beard, or moustache, to have high-pitched voices and several other characters which separate them from normal men.

The growth of organs and structures so remote from the sex-organs, as, e.g., the larnyx, have been found to be influenced by the chemical stimulus of secretions from the sex-organs and their subsidiary glands. These secretions are not passed out through external ducts but enter the blood system *directly*. Such secretions passing straight from the ductless glands into the vascular system are of very great importance in almost all our bodily functions. They have recently been much studied, and the general name of *Hormones* given to them by Starling.[1] The idea that some particular secretions or 'humours' are connected with each of the internal organs of the body, is a very ancient one; but we have even yet only the vaguest and most elementary knowledge of a few of the many miracles performed by these subtle chemical substances. Thus we know that the stimulus of food in the stomach sends a chemical substance from one ductless gland in the digestive system chasing through the blood to another gland which prepares a different digestive secretion further on. We know that the thyroid gland in the neck swells and contracts in very sensitive relation with the sex-organs; we know that some chemical secretion from the developing embyro, or the tissue in which it grows, sends its chemical stimulus to the distant mammary glands of the mother; we know that if the ovaries of a girl or the testes of a boy are completely cut out, the far-reaching influences their hormones would have exerted are made evident by the numerous changes in the system and departures from the normal, which result from their lack.

But we do *not* know, for physiologists have not yet studied the degree and character of the immense stimulus of sex-life and experience on the glands of the sex-organs, or how they affect the whole of the human being's life and powers.

The 'Mendelians' and the 'Mutationists,' who both tend to lay so much (and I think such undue) stress on morphological hereditary factors, seem at present to have the ear of the public more than the physiologists. But it is most important that every grown up man and woman should know that through the various chemical substances or 'messengers' (which Starling called the hormones) there is an extremely rapid, almost immediate, effect on the activities of organs in remote parts of the body, due to the influences exerted on one or other internal organ.

It is therefore clear that any influences exerted on such profoundly important organs as those connected with sex must have far-reaching results in many unexpected fields.

What must be taking place in the female system as a result of the completed sex act?

[1] See Prof. Ernest H. Starling's Croonian Lecture to the Royal Society, 1905.

It is true that in coitus woman has but a slight external secretion, and that principally of mucus. But we have no external signs of all the complex processes and reactions going on in digestion and during the production of digestive secretions. When, as is the case in orgasm, we have such intense and apparent nervous, vascular and muscular reactions, it seems inevitable that there must be correspondingly profound internal correlations. Is it conceivable that organs so fundamentally placed, and whose mere existence we know affects the personal characters of women, could escape physiological result from the intense preliminary stimulus and acute sensations of an orgasm?

To ask this question is surely to answer it. It is to my mind inconceivable that the orgasm in woman as in man should not have profound physiological effects. Did we know enough about the subject, many of the 'nervous breakdowns' and neurotic tendencies of the modern woman could be directly traced to the partial stimulation of sexual intercourse without its normal completion which is so prevalent in modern marriage.

This subject, and its numerous ramifications, are well worth the careful research of the most highly-trained physiologists. There is nothing more profound, or of more vital moment to modern humanity as a whole, than is the understanding of the sex nature and sex needs of men and women.

I may point out as a mere suggestion that the man's sex-organs give rise to *external* and also to *internal* secretions. The former only leave the glands which secrete them as a result of definite stimulus; the latter appear to be perpetually exuded in small quantities and always to be entering and influencing the whole system. In women we know there are corresponding perpetual internal secretions, and it seems evident to me that there must be some internal secretions which are only released under the definite stimulus of the whole sex-act.

The English and American peoples, who lead the world in so many ways, have an almost unprecedentedly high proportion of married women who get no satisfaction from physical union with their husbands, though they bear children, and may in every other respect appear to be happily married.

The modern civilised neurotic woman has become a by-word in the Western world. Why?

I am certain that much of this suffering is caused by the *ignorance* of both men and women regarding not only the inner physiology, but even the obvious outward expression, of the complete sex-act.

Many medical men now recognise that numerous nervous and other diseases are associated with the lack of physiological relief for natural or stimulated sex feelings in women. Ellis[1] quotes the opinion of an Austrian gynecologist who said that, 'of every hundred women who come to him with uterine troubles, seventy suffer from congestion of the womb, which he regarded as due to incomplete coitus.' While a writer in a recent number of the *British Medical Journal*[2] published some cases in which quite serious nervous diseases in wives were put right when their husbands were cured of too hasty ejaculation.

Sleep, concerning which I began this chapter, is but one of innumerable indications of inner processes intimately bound up with the sex-reactions. When the sex-rite is, in every sense, rightly performed, the healing wings of sleep descend both on the man and on the woman in his arms. Every organ in their bodies is influenced and stimulated to play its part, while their spirits, after soaring in the dizzy heights of rapture, are wafted to oblivion, thence to return gently to the ordinary plains of daily consciousness.

---

[1] H. Ellis. 'Sex in Relation to Society,' 1910, p. 551.
[2] See Porosz, *British Medical Journal*, April 1, 1911, p. 784.

CHAPTER VII

MODESTY AND ROMANCE

A person can therefore no more promise to love or not to love than he can promise to live long. What he can promise is to take good care of his life and of his love.—ELLEN KEY.

ARTISTS clearly, and poets in veiled language, have in all ages, expressed the glory of the naked human body. Before the Venus of Milo in her Paris home, even the empty-headed and ridiculously-dressed creatures of fashion stand for a moment with a catch in the throat and a sense that here is something full of divine secrets. One day, when I was doing my reverence before this ancient goddess, drinking in strength and happiness from the harmonies of her curves, a preposterously corsetted doll came up to the statue, paused, and said with tears in her voice to the man beside her: 'Hasn't she got the *loveliest* figure!'

If cold marble so stirs us, how much more the warmth and vitality of living beauty! Any well-formed young man or woman is immeasurably more graceful when free from the clinging follies of modern dress, while a beautiful woman's body has a supernal loveliness at which no words short of a poetic rapture can even hint. Our race has so long neglected the culture of human beauty that a sad proportion of mature men and women are unattractive; but most young people have the elements of beauty, and to them chiefly this book is addressed.

A young man or woman perfectly naked *cannot* be tawdry. The fripperies, the jagged curves and inharmonious lines and colours of the so-called 'adornments' are surmounted, and the naked figure stepping from their scattered pile is seen in its utter simplicity. How charming even the raggedest little street urchins become when they leave their rags on the bank and plunge into the water!

It is therefore not surprising that one of the innumerable sweet impulses of love should be to reveal, each to each, this treasure of living beauty. To give each other the right to enter and enjoy the sight which most of all sights in the world draws and satisfies the artist's eyes.

This impulse, however, is, on the part of the woman, swayed by two at least of the natural results of her rhythmic tides. For some time during each month, age-long tradition that she is 'unclean,' coupled with her obvious requirements, have made her withdraw herself from even her husband's gaze. But, on the other hand, there regularly come times when her body is raised to a higher point of loveliness than usual by the rounding and extra fullness of the breasts. (This is one of the regular physiological results of the rhythmic processes going on within her.) Partly or wholly unconscious of the brilliance and full perfection of her beauty, she yet delights in its gentle promptings to reveal itself to her lover's eyes when he adores. This innocent, this goddess-like self-confidence retreats when the natural ebb of her vitality returns.

How fortunate for man when these sweet changes in his lover are not coerced into uniformity! For man has still so much of the ancient hunter in his blood that beauty which is always at hand and ever upon its pedestal must inevitably attract him far less than the elusive and changing charms of rhythmic life. In the highly-evolved and cultivated woman, who has wisdom enough not to restrict, but to give full play to the great rhythms of her being, man's polygamous instinct can be satisfied and charmed by the ever-changing aspects of herself which naturally come uppermost. And one of her natural phases is at times to retreat, to experience a profound sex indifference, and passionately to resent any encroachment on her solitude.

This is something woman too often forgets. She has been so thoroughly 'domesticated' by man that she feels too readily that after marriage she is all his. And by her very docility to his perpetual demands, she destroys for him the elation, the palpitating thrills and surprises, of the chase.

In the rather trivial terms of our sordid modern life, it works out in many marriages somewhat as follows: The married pair share a bedroom, and so it comes about that the two are together not only at the times of delight and interest in each other, but during most of the unlovely and even ridiculous proceedings of the toilet. Now it may enchant a man once—perhaps even twice—or at long intervals—to watch his goddess screw her hair up into a tight and unbecoming knot and soap her ears. But it is inherently too unlovely a proceeding to retain indefinite enchantment. To see a beautiful woman floating in the deep, clear water of her bath—that may enchant for ever, for it is so lovely, but the unbeautiful trivialities essential to the daily toilet tend only to blur the picture and to dull the interest and attention that should be bestowed on the body of the loved one. Hence, ultimately, everyday association in the commonplace daily necessities tends to reduce the keen pleasure each takes in the other. And hence, inevitably and tragically, though stealthily and unperceived, to reduce the keenness of stimulation the pair exert on each other, and thus to lower their intensity of the consummation of the sex act, and hence to lower its physiological value.[1]

In short, the overcoming of her personal modesty, which is generally looked on as an essential result in marriage where the woman becomes wholly the man's, has generated among our women a tradition that before their husbands they can perform any and all of the details of personal and domestic duties. Correspondingly, they allow the man to be neglectful of preserving some reticence before them. This mutual possession of the lower and more elementary experiences of life has been, in innumerable marriages, a factor in destroying the mutual possession of life's higher and more poetic charms.

[1] A quotation from Thomas* (p. 112 of William Thomas' book 'Sex and Society,' 1907, Pp. 314) is here very apt, though he had been speaking not of man, but of the love play and coyness shown by female birds and animals.

'We must also recognise the fact that reproductive life must be connected with violent stimulation, or it would be neglected and the species would become extinct; and, on the other hand, if the conquest of the female were too easy, sexual life would be in danger of becoming a play interest and a dissipation, destructive of energy and fatal to the species. Working, we may assume, by a process of selection and survival, nature has both secured and safeguarded reproduction. The female will not submit to seizure except in a high state of nervous excitation (as is seen especially well in the wooing of birds), while the male must conduct himself in such a way as to manipulate the female; and, as the more active agent, he develops a marvelous display of technique for this purpose. This is offset by the coyness and coquetry of the female, by which she equally attracts and fascinates the male and practises upon him to induce a corresponding state of nervous excitation.'

And woman's beauty wanes too often more through neglect than through age. The man, with the radiant picture of his bride blurred by the daily less lovely aspects, may cease to remind her by acts of courtship that her body is precious. But many men by whom each aspect of their wives is noted, are often hurt by woman's stupidity or neglect of herself. Women lose their grace of motion by relying on artificial bones and stiffenings, and clog their movements with heavy and absurdly fashioned garments. They forget how immeasurably they can control not only their clothed appearance but the very structure of their bodies by the things they eat and do, by the very thoughts they think.

A wise man once said that a woman deserved no credit for her beauty at sixteen, but beauty at sixty was her own soul's doing. I would that all the world so thirsted for beauty that we moulded the whole race into as lovely forms as the Greeks created.

In this respect I am inclined to think that man suffers more than woman. For man is still essentially the hunter, the one who experiences the desires and thrills of the chase, and dreams ever of coming unawares upon Diana in the woodlands. On the other hand, the married woman, having once yielded all, tends to remain passively in the man's companionship.

Though it may appear trivial beside the profound physiological factors considered in recent chapters, I think that, in the interests of husbands, an important piece of advice to wives is: Be always escaping. Escape the lower, the trivial, the sordid. So far as possible (and this is far more possible than appears at first, and requires only a little care and rearrangement in the habits of the household) ensure that you allow your husband to come upon you only when there is delight in the meeting. Whenever the finances allow, the husband and wife should have separate bedrooms. No soul can grow to its full stature without spells of solitude. A married woman's body and soul should be essentially her own, and that can only be so if she has an inviolable retreat. But at the same time the custom of having separate rooms should not mean, as it often does, that the husband only comes to his wife's room when he has some demand to make upon her. Nothing is more calculated to inhibit all desire for union in a sensitive wife than the knowledge of what her husband wants when he comes, however lovingly, to her side. Every night, unless something prevents, there should be the tender companionship and whispered intimacies which are, to many people, only possible in the dark. The 'good-night' should be a time of delightful forgetting of the outward scars of the years, and a warm, tender, perhaps playful exchange of confidences. This is not incompatible with what has been said in the previous chapters, and when this custom is maintained it overcomes the objection some people make to separate rooms as a source of estrangements.

CHAPTER VIII

ABSTINENCE

How intoxicating indeed, how penetrating—like a most precious wine—is that love which is the sexual transformed by the magic of the will into the emotional and spiritual! And what a loss on the merest grounds of prudence and the economy of pleasure is its unbridled waste along physical channels! So nothing is so much to be dreaded between lovers as just this—the vulgarisation of love—and this is the rock upon which marriage so often splits.—EDWARD CARPENTER.

AND because marriage so often splits upon this rock, or because men and women have in all ages yearned for spiritual beauty, there have been those who shut themselves off from all the sweet usages of the body. In the struggle of man to gain command over his body, and in the slow and often backsliding evolution of the higher love, there is no doubt that humanity owes much to the ascetic. But this debt is in the past. We are now gaining control of the lower forces, we are winning knowledge of the complex meanings and the spiritual transformations of our physical reactions, and in the *future* the highest social unit will be recognised to be the pair, fused in love so that all human potentialities are theirs, as well as the higher potentialities which only perfect love can originate.

Yet, as we live to-day, with still so many remnants of the older standards within and upon us, we must endeavour to understand the ascetic. He (less often she) is by no means seldom one of the products of marriage. It not infrequently happens that after a love-marriage and some years of what is considered happiness, the man or woman may withdraw from the sex-life, often looking down upon it, and considering that they have reached a higher plane by so doing. But such people seldom ask themselves if, while they lived it, they reached the highest possible level of the sex-life.

One of the most famous instances of the married ascetic is Tolstoy, whose later opinion was that the *highest* human being completely inhibits his sex-desires and lives a celibate life. Ascetics, however, seldom have much knowledge of human physiology, and it seems to me that, with all their fine and religious fervour, they often lack the mysticism necessary for the full realisation of the meaning and potentialities of the new creation resulting from man's and woman's highest union. Doubtless if for an hour we were to take the place of the individual chemical atoms of Oxygen or of Hydrogen, we could have no inkling of the physical properties of the water-drop they together form.

Christianity, like most religions, had a strong wave of asceticism early in its history. While there was, as there still is, a harsh asceticism which is hostile to the other sex, it is of much interest to see that there was also a romantic asceticism which, while revolting from the sensuality of the pagan contemporaries, did not entirely prohibit the charms and pleasures of mutual companionship. Thus, in a mutilated form, it seems these early Christian ascetics gained some of the immaterial benefits of marriage. Ellis* (Vol. 6, 'Sex in Relation to Society,' 1910) gives an interesting account of these ascetic love-unions:

'Our fathers,' Chrysostom begins ('Against those who keep Virgins in their Houses'), 'only knew two forms of sexual intimacy, marriage and fornication. Now a third form has appeared: men introduce young girls into their houses and keep them there permanently, respecting their virginity. What,' Chrysotom asks, 'is the season? It seems to me that life in common with a woman is sweet, even outside conjugal union and fleshly commerce. That is my feeling; and perhaps it is not my feeling alone; it may also be that of these men. They would not hold their honour so cheap nor give rise to such scandals if this pleasure were not violent and tyrannical. . . . That there should really be a pleasure in this which produces a love more ardent than conjugal union may surprise you at first. But when I give you the proofs you will agree that it is so.' The absence of restraint to desire in marriage, he continues, often leads to speedy disgust, and even apart from this, sexual intercourse, pregnancy, delivery, lactation, the bringing up of children, and all the pains and anxieties that accompany these things, soon destroy youth and dull the point of pleasure. The virgin is free from these burdens. She retains her vigour and her youthfulness, and even at the age of forty may rival the young nubile girl. 'A double ardour thus burns in the heart of him who lives with her, and the gratification of desire never extinguishes the bright flame which ever continues to increase in strength.' Chrysostom describes minutely all the little cares and attentions which the modern girls of his time required, and which these men delighted to expend on their virginal sweethearts whether in public or in private. He cannot help thinking, however, that the man who lavishes kisses and caresses on a woman whose virginity he retains is putting himself somewhat in the position of Tantalus. But this new refinement of tender chastity, which came as a delicious discovery to the early Christians who resolutely thrust away the licentiousness of the pagan world, was deeply rooted, as we discover from the frequency with which the grave Fathers of the Church, apprehensive of scandal, felt called upon to reprove it, though their condemnation is sometimes not without a trace of secret sympathy.

Thus Jerome, in his letter to Eustochium, refers to those couples who 'share the same room,' often even the same bed, and call us suspicious if we draw any conclusions; while Cyprian (*Epistola*, 86) is unable to approve of those men he hears of, one a deacon, who live in familiar intercourse with virgins, even sleeping in the same bed with them, for, he declares, the feminine sex is weak and youth is wanton.

The harsh ascetic, however, is the one the word ascetic most generally conjures up. Even if he accomplishes miracles of self-restraint, and subdues desire, he is often weakened rather than strengthened by his determination to flout nature. Save only in the truly great, there is a warping and narrowing which results from coercing beyond the limits of reason the desires which were implanted in Adam and Eve when they were told to be fruitful and multiply.

As Ellen Key says ('Love and Marriage'):

Those ascetics who recommend only self-control as a remedy for the mastery of sexual instinct, even when such control becomes merely obstructive to life, are like the physician who tried only to drive the fever out of his patient: it was nothing to him that the sick man died of the cure.

But these ascetics may have arrived at their fanaticism by two different paths. One group—which includes most of the female ascetics—hates Cupid because he has never shown to them any favour.

The other group—embracing the majority of male ascetics—curse him because he never leaves them in peace.

Approaching the subject in a more modern and scientific attitude of impartial inquiry, the medical man can produce an imposing list of diseases more or less directly caused by abstinence both in men and in women. These diseases range from neuralgia and 'nerves' to (in women) fibroid growths. And it is well worthy of remark that these diseases may be present when the patient (as have many unmarried women) has no idea that the sex-impulse exists unmastered.

Thus the ascetic and the profligate (whether or not in *legal* marriage) have both to run the gauntlet of disease. There is, however, no disease I know of which is caused by the normal and mutually happy marriage relation—a relation which, certainly to most, has positive healing and vitalising power.

The profound truth which is perceived by the ascetics is that the creative energy of sex and can be *transformed* into other activities. This truth should never be lost sight of in marriage; where between the times of natural, happy, and also stimulating exercise of the sex-functions, the periods of complete abstinence should be opportunities for transmuting the healthy sex-power into work of every sort.

CHAPTER IX

CHILDREN

I am for you, and you are for me,
Not only for your own sake, but for others' sakes,
Envelop'd in you sleep greater heroes and bards,
They refuse to awake at the touch of any man but me.

WALT WHITMAN.*

THE Mystic in his moment of enlightenment attains through the flux of his personality the realisation of oneness with the divine forces of the Universe.

To ordinary men and women, however, this mystical ecstasy is unknown, and the ordinary human consciousness is far more aware of its separateness than of its oneness with the vital forces of creation. Yet the glow of half swooning rapture in which the mystic's whole being melts and floats in the light of the divine force is paralleled in the rapture of lovers.

When two who are mated in every respect burn with the fire of the innumerable forces within them, which set their bodies longing towards each other with the desire to inter-penetrate and to encompass one another, the fusion of joy and rapture is not purely physical. The half swooning sense of flux which overtakes the spirit in that eternal moment at the apex of rapture sweeps into its flaming tides the whole essence of the man and woman, and as it were, the heat of the contact vapourises their consciousness so that it fills the whole of cosmic space. For the moment they are identified with the divine thoughts, the waves of eternal force, which to the Mystic often appear in terms of golden light.

From their mutual penetration into the realms of supreme joy the two lovers bring back with them a spark of that light which we call life.

And unto them a child is born.

This is the supreme purpose of nature in all her enticing weft of complex factors luring the two lovers into each other's arms. Only by the fusion of two can the new human life come into being, and only by creating a new life in this way can we hand on the torch which lights our consciousness in the sphere of matter.

This mystical and wonderful fact has never yet found the poet to sing its full glory. But in the hearts of all who have known true love lies the realisation of the sacredness that is theirs when they are in the very act of creation.

Were our bodies specifically organised for this supreme purpose, two human beings would only pass through the sacred fire of mutual fusion in order to create a new life. But, however far our spirits have evolved, our bodies are composed of matter which bears the imprint of the many past phases through which we have reached our present position. And because in the world of the lower animals there is an immense wastage of all the young lives created, and it is necessary that myriads should be conceived in order that a small number should reach maturity, so in our bodies (specialised though they are in comparison with the lower animals) both sexes still produce a far larger number of germs awaiting fertilisation than can be actually fructified and imbued with individual life. So profoundly has the course of our history been stamped upon us that each germ, unaware of its own futility if it reaches maturity at an unpropitious moment is just as insistent in its development as the favoured one which follows out the full natural course of its career and gives rise to a new individual.

It is utterly impossible, organised as our bodies are at present, for us to obey the dictates of theologians and refrain from the destruction of potential life. The germ cells of the woman, though immeasurably less numerous than the male germ cells (the sperm) yet develop uselessly over and over again in every celibate as well as in every married woman. While myriads of sperm cells are destroyed even in the process of the act which does ensure fertilisation of the woman by the single favoured sperm. If the theologians really mean what they say, and demand the voluntary effort of complete celibacy from all men, save for the purpose of procreation, this will *not* achieve their end of preventing the destruction of all potential life; and the monthly loss of unfertilised egg-cells by women is beyond all the efforts of the will to curb. Nature, not man, arranged the destruction of potential life against which ascetic Bishops rage.

If, then, throughout the greater part of their lives the germinal cells of both sexes inevitably disintegrate without creating an embryo, there can be nothing wrong in selecting the most favourable moment possible for the conception of the first of these germinal cells to be endowed with the supreme privilege of creating a new life.

What generally happens in marriage where this is not thought of is that one of the very earliest unions results in the fertilisation of the wife, so that the young pair have a baby nine months, or a little more, after marriage.

Whereas, were they wise and did they realise the full significance of what they were doing, they would allow at least six months or a year to elapse before beginning the supreme task of their lives, the burden of which falls mainly upon the woman.

For many reasons it is more ideal to have the children spontaneously and early; but if economic conditions are hard, as they so often are in 'civilised' life, it may be better to marry and defer the children rather than not to marry.

If the pair married very young, and before they could afford to support children, they might wait several years with advantage. An exceptional case is one of the happiest marriages I know. The pair married while they were young students in the University, and fourteen years later they had their first child, a splendidly healthy boy. Though such a long interval is certainly not to be universally recommended, as it is said that it may result in sterility, in this instance it was triumphantly better for the two to have lived normally satisfied happy lives than to have waited for fourteen years and risked the man's 'fall.'

There are many reasons, both for their own and for the child's sake, why the potential parents should take the wise precaution of delay, unless owing to special circumstances they cannot expect to live together uninterruptedly.

The child, conceived in rapture and hope, should be given every material chance which the wisdom and love of the parents can devise. And the first and *most* vital condition of its health is that the mother should be well and happy and free from anxiety while she bears it.

The tremendous and far-reaching effects of marriage on the woman's whole organism make her less fitted to bear a child at the very commencement of marriage than later on, when the system will have adjusted itself to its new conditions.

Not only for the sake of the child, however, should the first conception be a little delayed, but also to secure the lasting happiness of the married lovers. It is generally (though perhaps not always) wise thoroughly to establish their relation to each other before introducing the inevitable dislocation and readjustment necessitated by the wife's pregnancy and the birth of a child.

In this book I am not speaking so much of the universal sex relation as to those who find themselves to-day in the highly civilised, artificial communities of English-speaking people: and in our present society there is little doubt that the early birth of a child demands much self-sacrifice and self-restraint from the man, one of the reflex vibrations of which is his undefinable sense of loss and separation from his bride. This has been confided to me by many men who have been generous enough to trust me with some of the secrets of their lives. Mr C. is typical of many others of his class.

He was quiet and refined, with a strong strain of romantic love, which was entirely centred in his bride. He was manly and sufficiently virile to feel the need of sex intercourse, but he was unaware (as are so many men) of the woman's corresponding need; and he did not give his wife any orgasm. She took no pleasure, therefore, in the physical act of union, which for her was so incomplete.

Very shortly after marriage she conceived, and a child was born ten months after the wedding day.

For two years after the birth of the child her vitality was so lowered that the sex-act was to her *so* repugnant that she refused her husband any union; and it was thus three years after their marriage before they met in anything like a normal way. By that time the long separation from sex-life, and the strain on the man, coupled with daily familiarity at home, had dimmed, if not

completely destroyed, his sense of romance. The natural stimulation each should exert on the other had faded, so that they never
experienced the mutual glow of rapture in their sex-union.

Another pair suffered similarly: Mr and Mrs D. were prevented for several years by the wife's real and fancied ill-health
from having any intercourse. When, after that time, she recovered
and passionately desired the true marriage relation, the husband
felt it to be impossible. To him it would have been, as he
expressed it, 'like raping his sister.'

Once such a thought has grown into a man's mind it is very
difficult 'to recapture the first fine early rapture.' And with the
loss of that early rapture the two lose, for the rest of their lives,
the irradiating joy which is priceless not only for its beauty, but
for the vitality with which its wings are laden.

On the other hand, if by waiting some months (or even years if
they are young) the mated pair have learnt to adjust themselves to
each other and have experienced the full possibilities of complete
love-making, the disturbance which is caused by the birth of the
child is in no sense a danger to their happiness, but is its crown
and completion.

A man once said to me—'One can endure anything for the sake
of a beloved wife.' But the *wife* is only utterly beloved when she
and her married lover have not only entered paradise together,
but when she fully realises, through insight gained by her own
experiences, the true nature of that of which she is depriving her
husband so long as her bodily condition makes sex-union with
him impossible.

Much has been written, and may be found in the innumerable
books on the sex-problems, as to whether a man and woman
should or should not have relations while the wife is bearing an
unborn child. In this matter experience is very various, so that it
is difficult or impossible to give definite advice without knowing
the full circumstances of each case.

When, however, we observe the admirable sanctity of the
pregnant females of the woodland creatures, and when we consider the extraordinary ignorance and disregard of woman's
needs which mark so many of our modern customs, we cannot

but think that the safe side of this debatable question must be in the complete continence of the woman for at least six months before the birth of the child. I have heard from a number of women, however, that they desire union urgently at this time; and from others that the thought of it is incredible.

Tolstoy strongly condemned any sex contact while the wife was pregnant or nursing, and blames the husband who 'puts upon her the unbearable burden of being at one and the same time a mistress, an exhausted mother, and a sickly, irritable, hysterical individual. And the husband loves her as his mistress, ignores her as a mother, and hates her for the irritability and hysteria which he himself has produced and produces.' His view is taken by many of our noblest men.

While the wife feels that she cannot allow her husband to enter the portals of her body when it has become the sacred temple of a developing life, she should also consider the perpetual strain which nature imposes upon him; and the tender and loving wife will readily find some means of giving him that physical relief which his nature needs.

The exquisite, unselfish tenderness which is aroused in a man by the sense of mental and spiritual harmony with a wife who sympathises with, because she understands, his needs is one of the loveliest things in marriage. The wife who knows how to waken this tenderness in a man raises him out of the self-centred slough in which so many men wallow unhappily.

With an ardent man, wholly devoted to his wife and long deprived of her, the time will come when it will be sufficient for him to be near her and caress her for relief to take place without any physical connection.

After the birth of the first child the health of the mother and of the baby both demand that there should be no hurried beginning of a second. *At least* a year should pass before the second little life is allowed to begin its unfolding, so that *a minimum* of about two years should elapse before the second child is born.

The importance of this, both for the mother and for the child, is generally adequately recognised by medical specialists, and some distinguished gynecologists advocate as much as three or five years between the births of successive children. While in the whole human relation there is no slavery or torture so horrible as coerced, unwilling motherhood, there is no joy and pride greater than that of a woman who is bearing the developing child of a man she adores. It is a serious reflection on our poisoned 'civilisation' that a pregnant woman should feel shame to appear in the streets. Never will the race reach true health till it is cured of its prurient sickness, and the prospective mother can carry her sacred burden as a priestess in a triumphal procession.

Of the innumerable problems which touch upon the qualities transmitted to the children by their parents, the study of which may be covered by the general term Eugenics, I shall here say nothing: nor shall I deal with the problems of birth and child-rearing. Many writers have considered these subjects, and my purpose in this book is to present aspects of sex-life which have been more or less neglected by others.

While throughout I have omitted the consideration of abnormalities, there is one condition which verges on the abnormal but yet touches the lives of some married people who are individually both normal and healthy, about which a few words need to be said.

It not infrequently happens that two healthy, loving people, for no apparent reason, seem unable to have a child.

The old-fashioned view was that the fault lay with the woman, and the reproach of being a barren woman is one which brought untold anguish to many hearts. It is now beginning to be recognised, however, that in a childless union the 'fault,' if fault it be, is as often the man's as the woman's, particularly where the husband is a brain worker in a city.

Though it is natural that there should not be the same joy for the pair in a child which had not arisen from their own supreme fusion, nevertheless, the man who is generous and broadminded might find much joy in a child of his wife's were the obtaining of this child not coupled with the yielding of her body to the embrace of another man, which is so generally and so naturally repugnant to a husband. The future possibilities of science here come in. Much interesting research has already been done on the growth of the young of various creatures without the ordinary fertilisation of the mother egg-cell. Then there are the experiments by the famous Dr Hunter* at the end of the eighteenth century, and more recent work. See, for instance, Heape,* in the 'Proceedings of the Royal Society, 1897,' and Marshall's* text-book of 'The Physiology of Reproduction, 1910.'

While in such an event as these discoveries adumbrate, the husband would have no bodily part in the heritage of the child, yet in the creation of its spirit he could play a profound part, the potentialities of which appear to be almost unrecognised by humanity.

The idea that the soul and character of the child can be in any degree influenced by the mental status of the mother during the months of its development as an embryo within her body, is apt to be greeted with pure scepticism—for it is difficult of proof, and repugnant to the male intellect, now accustomed to explain life in terms of chemistry.

Yet all the wisest mothers whom I know vary only in the degree of their belief in this power of the mother. All are agreed in believing that the spiritual and mental condition and environment of the mother does profoundly affect the character and the mental and spiritual powers of the child.

An interesting fact which strengthens the woman's point of view, is quoted (though not in this connection) by Marshall,[1] who says: 'It has been found that immunity from disease may be acquired by young animals being suckled by a female which had previously become immune, the antibody to the disease being absorbed in the ingested milk.' This particular fact is explainable in terms of chemistry; but it seems to me more than rash for anyone in these days of hormones from ductless glands, to deny the possibility of mental states in the mother generating 'chemical messengers,' which may impress permanent characters in the physiological reactions of the developing child. Ellis* says (Vol. 6, 'Sex in Relation to Society,' 1910): 'The mother is the child's supreme parent, and during the period from conception to birth

[1] See p. 566 of the text-book on 'The Physiology of Reproduction,' pp. xvii, 706, 1910.

the hygiene of the future man can only be affected by influences which work through her.'

And Alfred Russel Wallace, the great naturalist, thought the transmission of mental influence neither impossible nor even very improbable.[1] I am convinced that it takes place all the time, moulding and influencing the hereditary factors.

Hence I suggest that the husband who is deprived of normal fatherhood may yet make the child of his wife's body partly his own, if his thoughts are with her intensely, supportingly, and joyously throughout the whole time of the unborn baby's growth. If he reads to her, plays beautiful music or takes her to hear it, and gives her the very best of his thoughts and aspirations, mystical though the conclusion may seem, he does attain an actual measure of fatherhood.

The converse is even more difficult, where the wife is really barren and the husband capable of having children with another woman. Then the attainment of children by the man is impossible without the collaboration of another woman in a manner not outwardly recognised by our laws and customs. Even if this is done, it is clear that to introduce the child of another woman into the home is demanding a much greater self-abnegation from the wife than is demanded from the husband in the situation we have just considered.

Many people whose ideals are very noble are yet strangely incapable of adapting the material acts of life to the real fulfilment of their ideals. Thus there is a section of our community which insists that there should be no restriction whatever of the number of children born to married people. They think any birth control immoral. They take their stand upon the statement that we have no right to destroy potential life. But if they would study a little human or animal physiology they would find that not only every celibate, but also every married man incessantly and inevitably wastes myriads of germs (see p. 50) which had the potentiality of fusion with an ovum, and consequently could have produced a child had opportunity been given them. For the supposed sake of

[1] See his letter to the scientific journal 'Nature' in the year 1893, August 24, pp. 389 and 390.

one or two of these myriad sperms which must naturally and inevitably die, they encourage the production of babies in rapid succession which are weakened by their proximity while they might have been sturdy and healthy had they been conceived further apart from each other.

Such people, while awake to the claims of the unborn, nay, even of the unconceived, are blind to the claims of the one who should be dearest of all to the husband, and for whose health and happiness he is responsible. A man swayed by archaic dogma will allow, even coerce, his wife to bear and bring forth an infant annually. Save where the woman is exceptional, each child following so rapidly on its predecessor, saps and divides the vital strength which is available for the making of the offspring. This generally lowers the vitality of each succeeding child, and surely even if slowly, may murder the woman who bears them.

Of course, the effects of this strain upon the woman vary greatly according to her original health and vitality, the conditions of her surroundings and the intensity of the family's struggle for food. A half-starved mother trying to bring up children in the foul air of city slums, loses, as a rule, far more of her family than a comfortable and well-fed woman in the country. Nevertheless, conditions are not everything; under the best conditions, the chances of death of the later children of a large family, which comes rapidly, are far greater than for the earlier children.

Dr Ploetz* found that while the death-rate of first-born infants is about 220 per thousand, the death-rate of the seventh-born is about 330, and of the twelfth-born is 597 per thousand. So that when 'Nature' has its way, and twelve children come to sap a woman's vitality, so little strength has she that nearly 60 per cent of these later ones die. What a waste of vitality! What a hideous orgy of agony for the mothers to produce in anguish death-doomed, suffering infants!

Forel ('The Sexual Question,' 1908) says: 'It seems almost incredible that in some countries medical men who are not ashamed to throw young men into the arms of prostitution, blush when mention is made of anti-conceptional methods. This false modesty, created by custom and prejudice, waxes indignant at innocent things while it encourages the greatest infamies.'

It is important to observe that Holland, the country which takes *most* care that children shall be well and voluntarily conceived, has increased its survival-rate, and has thereby, not diminished, but increased its population, and has the lowest infant mortality in Europe. While in America, where the outrageous 'Comstock Laws'* confuse wise scientific prevention with illegal abortion and label them both as 'obscene,' thus preventing people from obtaining decent hygienic knowledge, horrible and criminal abortion is more frequent than in any other country.

It should be realised that all the proper, medical methods of controlling pregnancy consist, not in destroying an already growing embryo, but in preventing the male sperm from reaching the unfertilised egg-cell. This may be done either by shutting the sperms away from the opening of the womb, or by securing the death of *all* (instead of the natural death of all but *one*) of the two to six hundred million sperms which enter the woman. Even when a child is allowed to grow in its mother, all these hundreds of millions of sperms are inevitably and naturally destroyed every time the man has an emission, and to add one more to these millions sacrificed by Nature is surely no crime! To kill quickly the ejaculated sperms which would otherwise die and decompose naturally, is a simple matter. Their minute and uncovered bodies are plasmolised in weak acid, such as vinegar and water, or by a solution of quinine, or by many other substances.

To those who protest that we have no right to interfere with the course of Nature, one must point out that the whole of civilisation, everything which separates man from animals, is an interference with what such people commonly call 'Nature.'

Nothing in the cosmos can be against Nature, for it all forms part of the great processes of the universe.

Actions differ, however, in their relative positions in the scale of things. Only those actions are worthy which lead the race onwards to a higher and fuller completion and the perfecting of its powers, which steer the race into the main current of that stream of life and vitality which courses through us and impels us forward.

It is a sacred duty of all who dare to hand on the awe-inspiring gift of life, to hand it on in a vessel as fit and perfect as they can fashion, so that the body may be the strongest and most beautiful instrument possible in the service of the soul they summon to play its part in the mystery of material being.

CHAPTER X

SOCIETY

Love is fed not by what it takes, but by what it gives, and that excellent dual love of man and wife must be fed also by the love they give to others.—EDWARD CARPENTER.

MAN, even the commonplace modern man, is romantic. He craves consciously or unconsciously for the freedom, the beauty, and the adventure which his forefathers found in their virgin forests. This craving, transmuted, changed out of recognition by civilised life and modern circumstances, is yet a factor not to be ignored in the relationship of the sexes.

The 'bonds of matrimony,' so often referred to with ribald laughter, touch, and perhaps secretly gall, even the most romantic and devoted husband. If to the sincere and friendly question: 'What is most difficult in married life for the man?' one gets the sincere and rueful answer—that answer may be summed up in the words 'perpetual propinquity.'

Of this, the wife, particularly if she be really in love, is seldom fully aware. If her husband is her true lover, his tenderness and real devotion will give him the wit to conceal it. But though by concealment he may preserve the unruffled surface of their happiness, yet the longing to be roving is not completely extinguished. In the true lover this unspoken, unconscious longing is perhaps less a desire to set out upon a fresh journey than a longing to experience again the exquisite joy of the return; to re-live the magic charm of the approach to the spot in which the loved one is living her life, into the sacred separateness of which the lover breaks, and, like the Prince by his kiss, to stir her to fresh activity.

As will be realised by those who have understood the preceding chapters, each coming together of man and wife, even if they have been mated for many years, should be a fresh adventure; each winning should necessitate a fresh wooing.

Yet what a man often finds so hard is to come to that wooing with full ardour and with that complete sense of romance which alone can render it utterly delightful, if the woman he is to woo has been in a too uninterrupted and prosaic relation with him in the meantime.

Most men, of course, have their businesses apart from their homes, but in the home lives of the great mass of middle-class people the Victorian tradition still too largely preponderates, and the mated pair bore or deaden each other during the daily routine.

To a very thoughtful couple whom I have known, so precious was the sense of romantic joy in one another that they endeavoured to prepetuate it by living in different houses.

Such a measure, however, is not likely to suit many people, particularly where there are childern. Yet even without bodily separation (which must always entail expense) or any measure of freedom not at everyone's command, much can be done to retain that sense of spritiual freedom in which alone the full joy of loving union can be experienced.

But even intellectual and spritiual freedom is often rendered impossible in present-day marriage.

The beautiful desire for ideal unity which is so strong in most hearts is perhaps the original cause of one of the most deadening features in many marriages. In the endeavour to attain the ideal unity, one or other partner consciously or unconsciously imposes his or her will and opinions first upon the wife or husband, and then upon the childern as they grow up.

The typical self-opinionated male which this course develops, while a subject for laughter in plays and novels, a laughter which hastens his extermination, is yet by no means extinct. In his less exaggerated form such a man may often be an idealist, but he is essentially an idealist of narrow vision. The peace, the unity, for which he craves is superficially attained; but it takes acuter eyes than his to see that it is attained not by harmonious intermingling, but by super-position and destruction.

I have known a romantic man of this type, apparently unaware that he was encroaching upon his wife's personality, who yet endeavoured not only to choose her books and her friends for her, but 'prohibited' her from buying the daily newspaper to which she had been accustomed for years before her marriage, saying that one newspaper was enough for them both, and blandly ignoring the fact that he took it with him out of the house before she had an opportunity of reading it. This man posed to himself more successfully than to others, not only as a romantic man, but as a model husband; and he reproached his wife for jeoparadising their perfect unity whenever she accepted an invitation in which he was not included.

On the other hand, in homes where the avowed desire is for the modern freedom of intellectual life for both partners, there is very frequently a bickering, a sense of disharmony and unrest that dispels the peace and the air of restful security which is an essential feature of a true home.

It is one of the most difficult things in the world for two people of different opinions to retain their own opinions without each endeavouring to convert or coerce the other, and at the same time to feel the same tender trust in the judgment of the other that each would have felt had they agreed.

It takes a generous and beautiful heart to see beauty and dignity in the attitude of a mate who is looking at the other side of a vital question.

But the very fact that it *does* take a beautiful and generous heart to do this thing proves it well worth the doing.

If the easier way is chosen and the two mutually conceal their views when they differ, or the stronger partner coerces the weaker into hiding those traits which give personality to an individual, the result is an impoverishing of both, and through that very fact, an impoverishment, a lowering of the love which both sought to serve.

In marriage each one dreams that he will find the Understander—the one from whom he may set out into the world in search of treasures of knowledge and experience, and before whom the spoils may be exhibited without thought of rivalry, and with the certainty of glad apprisal. Treasures, dear to our own hearts but of no value to others, should here find appreciation, and here the tender super-sensitive germ of an idea may be watered and tended till its ripe beauty is ready to burst upon the world.

As marriage is at present such tenderness and such stimulating appreciation is much more likely to come from the woman to the man and his work than from the man to the woman. For too long have men been accustomed to look upon woman's views, and in particular on her intellectual opinions, as being something demanding at the most a bland humouring beneath the kindest smiles.

Even from the noblest man, the woman of sensitive personality to-day feels an undercurrent as of surprised congratulation when she has anything to say worth his *serious* attention outside that department of life supposed to belong to her 'sphere.' Thus man robs his wedded self of a greatness which the dual unity might reach.

But in marriage the mutual freedom and respect for opinion, vitally important though it be, is not sufficient for the full development of character. Life demands ever-widening interests. Owing partly to the differentiation of many types of individuals due to the specialisation of civilisation, which interests thoughtful individuals, and partly to the transmutation of his old vagrant instinct, man increasingly desires to touch and to realise the lives of his fellows. In the lives of others our hearts and understandings may find perpetual adventures into the new and strange.

Individual human beings, even the noblest and most complex yet evolved, have but a share of the innumerable faculties of the race. Hence even in a supremely happy marriage, which touches, as does the mystic in his raptures, a realisation of the whole universe, there cannot lie the *whole* of life's experience. Outside the actual lives of the pair there must always be many types of thought and many potentialities which can only be realised in the lives of other people.

In the complete human relation friends of all grades are needed, as well as a mate. Marriage, however, in its present form is too often made to curtail the enjoyment of intimate friendships. The reason for this is partly the social etiquette, which, though discarded in the highest levels of society, still lingers in many circles, of inviting the husband and the wife together upon all social occasions. It is true that they are separated at the dinner table, but they are always within the possibility of earshot of each other, which very often deadens their potentialities for being entertaining. The mere fact of being overheard repeating something one may have already said elsewhere is sufficient to prevent some people from telling their best stories, or from expressing their real views upon important matters.

And, still more serious barrier to joy, so primitive, so little evolved are we even yet, there is in most human beings a strong streak of sex-jealousy. For either mate to be allowed to go out uncriticised into the world, is to demand, if not more than the other is willing to give, at least a measure of trust which by its rarity appears nowadays as something conspicuously fine.

Jealousy, which is one of the most frequent shadows cast by the blight of love, is very apt to sow a distrust in one which makes a normal life for the other partner impossible.

It is hard to say in which sex the feeling is more strongly developed. It takes special forms under different circumstances, and if a nature is predisposed towards it, it is one of the most difficult characteristics to eradicate.

Custom, and generations of traditions, seem to have imprinted on our race the false idea that marital fidelity is to be strengthened by coercive bonds. We are slowly growing out of this, and nowadays in most books giving advice to young wives there is a section telling them that a man should be allowed his men friends after marriage.

But this is not enough. There should be complete and unquestioning trust on both sides. The man and the woman should each be free to go unchallenged by a thought on solitary excursions, or on visits, weekends or walking tours, without the possibility of a breath of jealousy or suspicion springing up in the heart of one or the other.

It is true that many natures are not yet ready for such trust, and might abuse such freedom. But the baser natures will always find a method of gratifying their desires, and are not likely to err more in trusted freedom than they would inevitably have done through secret intrigues if held in jealous bondage.

While, on the other hand, it is only in the fresh unsullied air of such freedom that the fullest and most perfect love can develop. In the marriage relation it is supremely true that only by loosening the bonds can one bind two hearts indissolubly together.

When they are sometimes physically apart married lovers attain the closest spiritual union. For with sensitive spirits—and they are the only ones who know the highest pinnacles of love—periods of separation and solitude can be revivifying and re-creative.

So great is the human soul that some of its beauty is hidden by nearness: it needs distance between it and the beholder to be perceived in its true perspective.

To the realisation of the beauty and the enjoyment of solitude, woman in general tends to be less awake than man. This, perhaps, is due to the innumerable generations during which the claims of her children and of domestic life have robbed her of Nature's healing gift.

Although it is merely incidental to the drama, yet to me the most poignant thing in Synge's beautiful play *Deirdré** is that she could feel inevitable tragedy when the first thought of something apart from herself crosses her lover's mind. Deirdré and her lover had been together for seven years in an unbroken and idyllic intimacy, and she feels that all is finished, and that her doom, the knell of their joy, had struck, when for the first time she perceived in him a half-formed thought of an occupation apart from her.

This ancient weakness of her sex must be conquered, and is being conquered by the modern woman.

While modern marriage is tending to give ever more and more freedom to each of the partners, there is at the same time a unity of work and interest growing up which brings them together on a higher plane than the purely domestic one which was so confining to the women and so dull to the men. Every year one sees a widening of the independence and the range of the pursuits of women: but still, far too often, marriage puts an end to woman's intellectual life. Marriage can never reach its full stature until women possess as much intellectual freedom and feedom of opportunity within it as do their partners.

That at present the majority of women neither desire freedom for creative work, nor would know how to use it, is only a sign that we are still living in the shadow of the coercive and dwarfing influences of the past.

In an interesting article on woman's intellectual work, W. Thomas (1907, 'Sex and Society') says:

The American woman, with the enjoyment of greater liberty, has made an approach toward the standards of professional scholarship, and some individuals stand at the very top in their university studies and examinations. The trouble with these cases is that they are either swept away and engulfed by the modern system of marriage, or find themselves excluded in some intangible way from association with men in the fullest sense, and no career open to their talents.

He sees clearly that this is but a passing phase in the development of our society, and he advocates a wider scope for the play of married women's powers.

The practice of an occupational activity of her own choosing by woman and a generous attitude towards this on the part of man, would contribute to relieve the strain and make marriage more frequently successful.

When woman naturally develops the powers latent within her, man will find at his side not only a mate, free and strong, but a desirable friend and an intellectual comrade.

The desire for freedom, both for physical and mental exploration and for experiences outside the sacred enclosure of the home, may at first sight appear to be conflicting and entirely incompatible with the ideal of closer and more perfect unity between the married pair. But this conflict is only apparent, though it is true that most writers have failed to realise this. Consequently in some sections of the writing and teaching of the 'advanced' schools there are claims only for increased freedom—a freedom to wander at will—a freedom in which the wanderer does not return to his fixed centre.

On the other hand there are those who realise principally the beauty of married unity, and, concentrating on the demand for the unity and extremest stability on the part of the married pair, are very apt to ignore the enriching flow of a wide life's experiences. They try to dam up the fertilising tide of life, and thus, though they are unconscious of what they are doing, they tend to reduce the richness and beauty of marriage.

It is for the young people of the new generation to realise that the two currents of longing which spring up within them—the longing for a full life-experience and the longing for a close union with a lifelong mate—are not incompatible, but are actually both essential parts of the more perfect and fuller beauty of the future that already seeks to find its expression in their lives.

Ellen Key ('Love and Marriage') seems to fear the widening of the married woman's life, and she writes as though the aspiration to do professional and intellectual work of a high order must dwarf and sterilise the mother in the married woman.

She writes of a more northerly people, the Scandinavians, and it may be true of her countrywomen, I do not know. But it is *not* essentially and universally true. I am writing of the English, the English of to-day, and though we also have among us that dwarfed and sterilised type of woman, she forms in our community a dwindling minority. The majority of our best women enter marriage and motherhood, or else long for a marriage more beautiful than the warped mockery of it that is offered them.

As Mrs Stetson* says ('Women and Economics'):

In the primal physical functions of maternity the human female cannot show that her supposed specialisation to these uses has improved her fulfilment of them, rather the opposite. The more freely the human mother mingles in the natural industries of a human creature, as in the case of the savage woman, the peasant woman, the working woman everywhere who is not overworked, the more rightly she fulfils these functions.

The more absolutely the woman is segregated to sex-functions only, cut off from all economic use and made wholly dependent on the sex-relation as means of a livelihood, the more pathological does her motherhood become. The over-development of sex caused by her economic dependence on the male reacts unfavourably on her essential duties. She is too female for the perfect motherhood!

The majority of our young women, I am convinced, have in them the potentiality of a full and perfected love. So, too, have the majority of our young men. For the best type of young man to-day is tired of polygamy; he has seen enough in his father's and friends' lives of the weariness of the sinister, secret polygamy, that hides itself and rots the race under the protecting cloak of the supposed monogamy of our social system.

But as things are at present in England, the young man who marries, however much he may be in love, is generally too ignorant (as has been indicated in the preceding chapters) to give his wife all her nature requires. Then, sooner or later, comes the sequence of disappointments which culminate in the longing for a fresh adventure.

As one young husband said to me, 'A decent man can't go on having unions with his wife when she obviously does not enjoy them,' and so he is forced to 'go elsewhere.' 'And they call us polygamists! We are not polygamists any longer. But marriage is a rotten failure,' was his verdict.

No. They are not polygamists, the finest young men of the present and of the future. Most men to-day are not in their heart of hearts polygamists, in spite of all the outward signs to the contrary; in spite of the fact that so few of them have remained faithful to one woman. But they are ignorant of the sex-laws and traditions, that sex-knowledge which was the heritage of much less civilised tribes, and so they have trampled and crushed out the very thing for the growth of which their hearts are aching.

Hence secretly (for in a marriage that is at least superficially happy the man seldom does this openly) the man begins to crave for another type of society and he 'goes elsewhere.' Not, it is true, to find, or even in the hope of finding, what he would get from a perfect marriage; but often to satisfy in some measure that yearning for fresh experience, for romance, and for that sense of fusion with another in the romantic experience which, even if it is only a delusion of the senses, is yet one of the most precious things life has to offer.

It is hard, indeed in many cases it seems impossible, for a good woman to understand what it is that draws her husband from her. Restricted by habit and convention in the exercise of her faculties, she is unaware of the ever-narrowing range of her interest and her powers of conversation. The home life tends to become that of a fenced pond, instead of a great ocean with innumerable currents. From the restricted and fenced, man's instinct is ever to escape. Man's opportunities for exploration in the cities are few, and the prostitute is one of the most obvious doors of escape into new experiences.

Women feel a so righteous and instinctive horror of prostitution, and regarding it they experience an indignation so intense, that they do not seek to understand the man's attitude.

The prostitute, however, sometimes supplies an element which is not purely physical, and which is often lacking in the wife's relation with her husband, an element of charm and mutual gaiety in pleasure.

If good women realised this, while they would judge and endeavour to eliminate prostitution no less strenuously, they might be in a better position to begin their efforts to free men from the hold that social disease has upon them.

It is perhaps impossible to find the beginning of a vicious circle, but the first step out of it must be the realisation that one is within it, and the realisation of some, at any rate, of its component parts.

Man, through prudery, through the custom of ignoring the woman's side of marriage and considering his own whim as marriage law, has largely lost the art of stirring a chaste partner to physical love. He therefore deprives her of a glamour, the loss of which he deplores, for he feels a lack not only of romance and beauty, but of something higher which is mystically given as the result of the complete union. He blames his wife's 'coldness' instead of his own want of art. Then he seeks elsewhere for the things she could have given him had he known how to win them. And she, knowing that the shrine has been desecrated, is filled with righteous indignation, though generally as blind as he is to the true cause of what has occurred.

Manifold and far-reaching, influencing the whole structure of society not only in this country, but in every country and at every time, have been the influences which have grown up from the root-fallacy in the marriage relation.

Then there is another cause for the dulling of a wife's bright charm—her inferior position in the eyes of the law. It is indeed a serious matter, as Jean Finot* says, 'that, under present conditions, the mistress keeps certain liberties which are denied to married women.'

The past and its history have been studied by many, and we may leave it. What concerns the present generation of young married people is to-day and the future. The future is full of hope. Already one sees beginning to grow up a new relationship between the units composing society.

In the noblest society love will hold sway. The love of mates will always be the supremest life experience, but it will no longer be an experience exclusive and warped.

The love of friends and children, of comrades and fellow-workers, will but serve to develop every power of the two who are mates. By mingling the greatness of their individual stature they can achieve together something that, had both or either been dwarfed and puny individuals, would have remained for ever unattainable.

The whole trend of the evolution of human society has been toward an increased coherence of all its parts, until at the present time it is already almost possible to say that the community has an actual life on a plane above that of all the individuals composing it: that the community, in fact, is a super-entity. It is through the community of human beings, and not in our individual lives, that we reach an ultimate permanence upon this globe.

When our relation to the community is fully realised, it will be seen that the health, the happiness, and the consequent powers of every individual, concern not only his own life, but also affect the whole community of which he is a member.

The happiness of a perfect marriage, which enhances the vitality of the private life, renders one not only capable of adding to the stream of the life-blood of the community in children, but by marriage one is also rendered a fitter and more perfect instrument for one's own particular work, the results of which should be shared by society as a whole, and in the tempering and finishing of which society plays a part.

Thus it is the concern of the whole community that marriage should be as perfect, and hence as joyous, as possible; so that the powers which should be set free and created for the purpose of the whole community should not be frittered away in the useless longing and disappointment engendered by ignorance, narrow restrictions, and low ideals.

In the world the happily mated pair should be like a great and beautiful light; a light not hid under a bushel, but one whose beams shine through the lives of all around them.

CHAPTER XI

THE GLORIOUS UNFOLDING

Let knowledge grow from more to more, but more of reverence
in us dwell.

TENNYSON.*

WE are surrounded in this world by processes and transmutations
so amazing that were they not taking place around us hourly they
would be scouted as impossible imaginings.

A mind must be dull and essentially lacking in wonderment
which, without amazement, can learn for the first time that the
air we breathe, apparently so uniform in its invisible unity, is in
reality composed of two principal, and several other, gases. The
two gases, however, are but mixed as wine may be with water, and
each gas by itself is a colourless air, visually like that mixture of
the two which we call the atmosphere.

Much greater is the miracle of the compositon of water. It is
made of only two gases, one of them a component of the air we
breathe, and the other similarly invisible and odourless, but far
lighter. These two invisible gases, when linked in a proportion
proper to their natures, fuse and are no longer ethereal and
invisible, but precipitate in a new substance—water.

The waves of the sea with their thundering power, the spark-
ling tides of the river buoying the ships, are but the transmuted
resultants of the union of two invisible gases. And this, in its
simplest terms, is a parable of the infinitely complex and amazing
transmutations of married love.

Ellis expresses the strange mystery of one of the physical sides
of love when he says:

What has always baffled men in the contemplation of sexual love is the
seeming inadequacy of its cause, the immense discrepancy between
the necessarily circumscribed regions of mucous membrane which is
the final goal of such love and the sea of world-embracing emotions to
which it seems the door, so that, as Remy de Gourmont has said, 'the

mucous membranes, by an ineffable mystery, enclose in their obscure folds all the riches of the infinite.' It is a mystery before which the thinker and the artist are alike overcome.

To me, however, the recent discoveries of physiology seem to afford a key which may unlock a chamber of the mystery and admit us to one of the halls of the palace of truth. The hormones (see pages 65–6) in each individual body pour from one organ and affect another, and thus influence the whole character of the individual's life processes. The visible secretions and the most subtle essences which pass during union between man and woman, affect the lives of each and are essentially vital to each other. As I see them, the man and the woman are each organs, parts, of the other. And in the strictest scientific, as well as in a mystical, sense they *together* are a single unit, an individual entity. There is a *physiological* as well as a spiritual truth in the words 'they twain shall be one flesh.'

In love it is not only that the yearning of the bonds of affinity to be satisfied is met by the linking with another, but that out of this union there grows a new and unprecedented creation.

In this I am not speaking of the bodily child which springs from the love of its parents, but of the super-physical entity created by the perfect union in love of man and woman. Together, united by the love bonds which hold them, they are a new and wondrous thing surpassing, and different from, the arithmetical sum of them both when separate.

So seldom has the perfection of this new creation been experienced, that we are still far short even of imagining its full potentialities, but that it must have mighty powers we dimly realise.

Youths and maidens stirred by the attraction of love, feel hauntingly and inarticulately that there is before them an immense and beautiful experience: feel as though in union with the beloved there will be added powers of every sort which have no measure in terms of the ordinary unmated life.

These prophetic dreams, if they are not true of each individual life, are yet true of the race as a whole. For in the dreams of youth to-day is a foreshadowing of the reality of the future.

So accustomed have we recently become to accept one aspect of organic evolution, that we tend to see in youth only a recapitulation of our race's history. The well-worn phrase 'Ontogeny repeats Phylogeny' has helped to concentrate our attention on the fact that the young in their development, in ourselves as in the animals, go through many phases which resemble the stages through which the whole race must have passed in the course of its evolution.

While this is true, there is another characteristic of youth: It is prophetic!

The dreams of youth, which each young heart expects to see fulfilled in its own life, seem so often to fade unfulfilled. But that is because the wonderful powers of youth are not supplied with the necessary tool—knowledge. And so potentialities, which could have worked miracles, are allowed to atrophy and die.

But as humanity orients itself more truly, more and more will the knowledge and experience of the whole race be placed at the disposal of all youth on its entry into life.

Then that glorious upspringing of the racial ideal, which finds its expression in each unspoiled generation of youth, will at last meet with a store of knowledge sufficient for its needs, and will find ready as a tool to its hand the accumulated and sifted wisdom of the race.

Then youth will be spared the blunders and the pain and the unconscious self-destruction that to-day leaves scarcely anyone untouched.

In my own life, comparatively short and therefore lacking in experience though it be, I have known both personally and vicariously so much anguish that might have been prevented by knowledge. This impels me not to wait till my experience and researches are complete, and my life and vital interest are fading, but to hand on at once those gleanings of wisdom I have already accumulated which may help the race to understand itself. Hence I conclude this little book, for, though incomplete, it contains some of the vital things youth should be told.

In all life activities, house-building, hunting or any other, where intellectual and oral tradition comes in, as it does with the human race, 'instinct' tends to die out. Thus the human mother is far less able to manage her baby without instruction than is a cat her kittens; although the human mother at her best has, in comparison with the cat, an infinitude of duties toward, and influences over, her child.

A similar truth holds in relation to marriage. The century-long following of various 'civilised' customs has not only deprived our young people of most of the instinctive knowledge they might have possessed, but has given rise to innumerable false and polluting customs.

Though many write on the art of managing children, few have anything to say about the art of marriage, save those who have some dogma, often theological or subversive of natural law, to proclaim.

Any fundamental truth regarding marriage is rendered immeasurably difficult to ascertain because of the immense ranges of variety in human beings, even of the same race, many of which result from the artificial conditions and the unnatural stimuli so prevalent in what we call civilisation. To attempt anything like a serious study of marriage in all its varieties would be a monumental work. Those who have even partially undertaken it have tended to become entangled in a maze of abnormalities, so that the needs of the normal, healthy, romantic person have been overlooked.

Each pair, therefore, has tended to repeat the blunders from which it might have been saved, and to stumble blindly in a maze of difficulties which are not the essential heritage of humanity, but are due to the unreasoning folly of our present customs.

I have written this book for those who enter marriage normally and healthily, and with optimism and hope.

If they learn its lessons they may be saved from some of the pitfalls in which thousands have wrecked their happiness, but they must not think that they will thereby easily attain the perfection of marriage. There are myriad subtleties in the adjustment of any two individuals.

Each pair must, using the tenderest and most delicate touches, sound and test each other, learning their way about the intricacies of each other's hearts.

Sometimes, with all the knowledge and the best will in the world, two who have married find that they cannot fuse their lives; of this tragedy I have not here anything to say; but ordinary unhappiness would be less frequent than it is were the tenderness of *knowledge* applied to the problem of mutual adjustment from the first day of marriage.

All the deepest and highest forces within us impel us to evolve an ever nobler and tenderer form of life-long monogamy as our social ideal. While the thoughtful and tenderhearted must seek, with ever greater understanding, to ease and comfort those who miss this joyful natural development, reformers in their zeal for side-issues must not forget the main growth of the stock. The beautiful sense for love in the hearts of the young should be encouraged, and they should have access to the knowledge of how to cultivate it, instead of being diverted by the clamour for 'freedom' to destroy it.

Disillusioned middle age is apt to look upon the material side of the marriage relation, to see its solid surface in the cold, dull light of everyday experience; while youth, irradiated by the glow of its dreams, is unaware how its aerial and celestial phantasies are broken and shattered when unsuspectingly brought up against the hard facts of physical reality.

The transmutation of material facts by celestial phantasies is to some extent within the power of humanity, even the imperfect humanity of to-day.

When knowledge and love together go to the making of each marriage, the joy of *that new unit, the pair* will reach from the physical foundations of its bodies to the heavens where its head is crowned with stars.

NOTE

While I believe that the charts I give of the Law of Periodicity of recurrence of desire truly represent the fundamental rhythm of average healthy women, it must be remembered that my theory is new, and every well-authenticated case for or against it will be valuable. I invite letters from those who can confirm, qualify, or correct my views from their own experience. To obtain scientific knowledge the largest possible number of individual cases must be studied. All communications will be treated with the strictest confidence.

Dr M. C. STOPES,
c/o Mr A. C. Fifield,*
13, Clifford's Inn, London, EC4.

APPENDIX

NOTE 1.—(See p. 35.)

For suffering and even death of unmated females, see *e.g.* MARSHALL, in *Quarterly Journal of Microscopical Science,** Vol. 48, 1904, p. 323.

PARSONS, in *British Medical Journal*, October, 1904.

NOTE 2.—(See p. 41.)

A frequent mistake (made even by gynaecologists) is to confuse menstruation with the 'period of desire,' which is generally called 'heat' in animals. Even in the most authoritative recent text books, such phrases as 'heat and menstruation' are very common, thus coupling heat and menstruation as though they were equivalents, while the older books quite explicitly look on the menstrual period in women as corresponding to desire of 'heat' in animals. This error has even been repeated very recently in the *Proceedings* of the Royal Society of Medicine.[1]

Some physiologists have studied this subject in several of the higher animals, and now realise that the time of desire is physiologically distinct from the phase which is represented by menstruation in women. It seems to be fairly well established that in women menstruation is caused by an internal secretion of the ovaries (*c.f.* pp. 65–6), and is not directly due to ovulation, though it must have some connection with it.[2]

The most that modern science appears to have attained is briefly summarised in the following quotation from Marshall ('The Physiology of Reproduction,' p. 69): 'According to Martin and certain other writers, the human female often experiences a distinct post-menstrual oestrus [Modern research has recognised a period when the female animal is ready for impregnation, which is called the oestrus and a preparatory series of physiologicol changes called the pro-estrous

---

[1] See Dr Raymond Crawfurd's mistaken statement that 'the identity of oestrus, or "heat" in the lower animals and of menstruation in the human female, admits of no doubt.' p. 62 *Proc.* Roy. Soc. Medicine, vol. 9, 1916.

[2] The best modern account of these complex subjects will be found in the advanced text-book, 'The Physiology of Reproduction,' pp. xvii, 706, by F. H. A. Marshall. Reference may be made to original papers by J. Beard in the Anat. Anzeiger. for 1897; and by Heape in the Philosophical Trans. Royal Society, 1894, 97.

phase.—M.C.S.], at which sexual desire is greater than at other times; so that, although conception can occur throughout the intermenstrual periods, it would seem probable that originally coition was restricted to definite periods of oestrus following menstrual or pro-estrous periods in women, as in females of other mammalia. On this point Heape write as follows: "This special time for oestrus in the human female has very frequently been denied, and, no doubt, modern civilisation and modern social life do much to check the natural sexual instinct where there is undue strain on the constitution, or to stimulate it at other times where extreme vigour is the result. For these reasons a definite period of oestrus may readily be interfered with, but the instinct is, I am convinced, still marked." '

In nearly all wild animals there is a definite period for sexual excitement, very commonly just at that time of the year which fits into the span of gestation, so that the young are born at the season which gives them the best chance to grow up. In animals the period of desire, the ovulation (or setting free of the female germ or unfertilised egg-cell) and the time of the birth of the young, are all co-related harmoniously. The male animal is only allowed to approach the female when the natural longing for union is upon her. Among human beings, the only race which seems to have long periods of sexual quiescence at all comparable with those natural to the animals are the Esquimaux, who appear to pass many months without any unions of the men and women.

EXPLANATORY NOTES

Stopes's minor errors of transcription from her sources have been silently corrected.

5 *Murray*: Jessie Margaret Murray (1867–1920), a pioneering woman doctor, qualified in 1909 and then took her MD in 1919. Her main fields of interest were the relationship between psychology and medicine and, later, psychoanalysis. She was the principal agent in the establishment of the Medico-Psychological Clinic in Brunswick Square, which encouraged the use of applied psychology in the treatment of medical conditions; one of the founders of the Society for the Study of Orthopsychics, a body which offered a broad scientific education as well as the study of applied and theoretical psychology, also an active member of the British Society for the Study of Sex Psychology.

8 *Starling*: E. H. Starling (1866–1927), distinguished physiologist whose *Principles of Human Physiology* (1st edn. 1912) was immensely influential. He was professor of Physiology, University College London, Stopes's own institution.

10 *Saleeby*: C. W. Saleeby (1878–1940), doctor and prolific writer on medicine, science, sociology, politics, and philosophy; a very committed eugenicist.

12 *St John*: Father Stanislaus St John SJ (1865–1943), son of a Baptist minister who, with his mother and younger brother, converted to Roman Catholicism when he was 12. Educated in Belgium, he entered the noviceship in 1884 and was ordained in 1898. After several years at Bristol, Tronchiennes, and St Helens, he joined the staff at Mount Street, London, the headquarters of the British province of the Society of Jesus, where he remained until 1922, after which he served in Osterley, Wardour, and Stamford Hill. He died of a heart attack during an air-raid alert in 1943.

19 *Carpenter*: Edward Carpenter (1844–1929), well-known literary and political figure and pioneering 'sexologist'. See also Introduction, pp. xxiv–xxvi, above.

Forel: A. H. Forel (1848–1931), Swiss scientist and psychiatrist; eugenicist and socialist; temperance campaigner and opponent of prostitution. See also Introduction, pp. xxx–xxxiii, above.

Stopes is almost certainly referring to chapter VIII of *The Sexual Question* here.

22 *AE in 'The Hero in Man'*: AE, the nom de plume of George William Russell (1867–1935), a leading figure in the Irish literary renaissance and the Irish national movement. *The Hero in Man* was a rather

mystical–religious essay admired by theosophists as well as Stopes. Diarmuid Russell's description of his father as 'a mixture of realistic hardheadedness and mysticism' is, in fact, not a bad description of Stopes (D. Russell, introduction to H. Summerfield (ed.), *G. W. Russell– A.E.: Selections from the Contributions to the 'Irish Homestead'*, vol. i (Gerrard's Cross, 1978), 1). See also Explanatory Note to p. 95, below and Introduction, pp. xviii–xx, above.

23 *'femmes incomprises'*: literally 'misunderstood or unappreciated women', that is, women who attribute their sexual and marital failures to the refusal of others to understand their real qualities. An ironic description.

26 *Key*: Ellen Key (1849–1926), celebrated Swedish feminist and political writer. Her work was particularly influential in the early twentieth century. See also Introduction, pp. xxvii–xxix, above.

27 *Herrick*: Robert Herrick (1591–1674), poet, follower of Ben Jonson; one of those known as 'cavalier poets'. He is lamenting the fact that he has, in effect, been unable to overcome 'women's "contrariness" '.

34 *Katherine Nelson*: not identified.

35 *'Conjugal Rights'* ... *Mr T. E. Paget writes*: it would be surprising if Stopes did not acquire these references from her mother.

37 *The Fundamental Pulse*: this chapter is unusual in *Married Love* in that it depends upon a form of individual research. Stopes rather muddied the water initially by arguing that the book, on the one hand, 'is less a record of research than an attempt to present in easily understandable form the clarified and crystallised results of long and complex investigations', and, on the other, that it was also 'based upon a very large number of first-hand observations' (p. 9). Elsewhere in the book she wrote that 'for many years men and women have confided to me the secrets of their lives' (p. 23)—implying that they had thereby provided her with a kind of database. Stopes certainly believed that her 'Law of Periodicity of Recurrence of Desire in Women' was a statement of physiological fact: though whether true of all women was to be determined. In *Married Love* she noted that she would in due course present her findings in the appropriate scientific literature; and at the end of the first edition she invited her women readers to send her details of their own cycles of sexual desire—a request eventually dropped in the seventh edition since she was already swamped with correspondence and hardly needed to incite any more.

Stopes criticizes Ellis and Marshall for relying upon received wisdoms in their discussions of the sexual cycle in women. They publish diagrams, 'but it is always the same old diagram' (p. 40). Stopes, however, argues that her Law is based upon first-hand experience: that of happily married women whose husbands had to be away for some time: 'Such women, yearning daily for the tender comradeship and nearness of their husbands, find, in addition, at particular times, an accession of longing for the close physical union of the final sex-act' (p. 39). Who and how many there were, we do not know. They certainly consisted of Stopes herself. Jessie Murray, Stopes's doctor-friend, appears to have been another. In her preface she wrote that 'Further observation is required to establish or disprove [Stopes's] theory of the normal sexual cycle in women, but my own observation certainly tends to confirm it' (p. 7). In fact, in her use of evidence, Stopes follows (in much briefer compass) the dominant contemporary models of sexology—typified, for example, by Ellis or Forel—which was to combine a synthesis of the existing literature with observational evidence drawn upon autobiography and the experience of lovers, friends, and acquaintances. It was a habit that discredited much early sexology and which the huge surveys of sexual behaviour undertaken after the Second World War were designed to correct. In the end, she appears not to have published her results in the scientific arena; and given how anecdotal they were this is not surprising.

Stopes concludes that women have 'fortnightly periods of [sexual] desire, arranged so that one period comes always just *before* each menstrual flow' (p. 42). It followed, she argues, that 'The mutually best regulation of intercourse in marriage is to have three or four days of repeated unions, followed by about ten days without any unions at all, unless some strong internal stimulus has stirred a mutual desire' (p. 52). There were inevitably caveats to this general rule. Some women usually feel only one peak of desire, but might feel a second 'when they are particularly well, or when they read exciting novels [and that does sound autobiographical], or meet the man they love at a time coinciding with the natural, but suppressed, time of desire'. She conceded that there were even women 'who feel the strongest desire actually during the menstrual flow' (p. 45).

Stopes was proud of her Law. Havelock Ellis thought it helpful and incorporated it into his later writing. Yet its significance lies not so much in its rightness or wrongness, coherence or incoherence, as in its assertion of the instinctive force and autonomy of women's sexual desire: 'a physical, a physiological state of stimulation which arises spontaneously and quite apart from any particular man. It is in truth the *creative* impulse, and is an expression of a high power of vitality' (p. 37). This is in itself a very strong argument. The Law must be seen, therefore, as one part of Stopes's attack on the view that 'nice' women feel (or acknowledge) no sexual desire; that in the art of love they are merely passive. But it also added weight to her argument that, since women not only had an independent sexuality, but sexual desires which were, like ovulation, cyclical, men had to adjust their own sexual behaviour to meet the desires of their wives—that sexual relations, like social relations, to be successful had to be mutual.

Ellis: Henry Havelock Ellis (1859–1939) trained as a doctor and prolific author and translator of German and French literature. Best known for his huge *Studies in the Psychology of Sex*. See also Introduction, p. xxvi, above.

37 *Windscheid*: probably F. Windscheid, a German physiologist, whose *Neuropatholigie und Gynäkologia* (1896) is still in print.

    Ellen Key: in the original text Ellen Key appears as Helen Key.

46 *Galabin*: A. L. Galabin (1843–1913), a distinguished physician and gynaecologist. *A Manual of Midwifery* (1st edn. London, 1886) was a standard text for many years.

54 *Karezza*: in the original text Stopes incorrectly calls Dr Alice B. Stockham 'Dr Alice B. Stockman'. Havelock Ellis wrote of Stockham: 'I once had a visit from Dr. Stockham, a simple and sensible person, but her book [*Karezza: Ethics of Marriage* (1896)] was described to me by Edward Carpenter, not altogether incorrectly, as, although containing much that is beautiful, "a farrago of absurdity" ' (Ellis, *Sex in Relation to Society* (1937 edn.), 432). Karezza is *coitus reservatus*, an arcane and exceptionally difficult form of contraception and/or love-making. Why Stopes should have introduced such an obscure, demanding, and unreliable technique into a book which was meant to be plain-speaking and for the wider public is a puzzle.

58 *The Way of God in Marriage*: Mary E. Teats, *The Way of God in Marriage: Essays upon Gospel and Scientific Purity* (London, 1906).

61 *He giveth His Beloved Sleep*: 'The Sleep' by Elizabeth Barrett Browning (1806–61), from *The Seraphim, and Other Poems* (1838).

71 *Thomas*: William Isaac Thomas (1863–1947), a distinguished anthropologist and physiologist now best known as the author (with Florian Znaniecki) of the *Polish Peasant in Europe and America: Monograph of an Immigrant Group* (Boston, 1918).

75 *Ellis*: in the original text the book is wrongly called *Sex and Society* and the date of publication is given as 1913 instead of 1910.

78 *Walt Whitman*: American poet (1819–92). These lines are from *Leaves of Grass*, stanza 20 'A Woman Waits for Me'. The opening lines to the stanza are perhaps more appropriate:

    A woman waits for me—she contains all, nothing is lacking
    Yet all were lacking, if sex were lacking, or if the moisture of the right
    man were lacking.

85 *Dr Hunter*: John Hunter (1728–93), celebrated surgeon, anatomist, scientist, and collector. Famous for his surgical technique as well as polymath.

    Heape: Walter Heape (1855–1929), biologist and physiologist. See also above, pp. xlviii–xlix.

    Marshall: F. H. A. Marshall (1878–1949), physiologist, demographer, and naturalist. *The Physiology of Reproduction* (1st edn. 1910) was, and is, a standard text.

    Ellis: see note to p. 37, above.

87 *Dr Ploetz*: not identified.

88 *'Comstock Laws'*: named after Anthony Comstock (1844–1915), Secretary of the New York Society for the Suppression of Vice, who persuaded the United States Congress in 1873 to pass legislation which made illegal the transmission of 'obscene' material through the postal service. In practice, the legislation was also used to prosecute the distribution of birth control literature. Margaret Sanger fled to England in 1915 to avoid conviction under this legislation: which occasioned her first meeting with Stopes (see Introduction, p. vii and n. 2, above). It was in England that Sanger wrote her famous attack on the laws, *Comstockery in America* (July 1915). The law was never repealed but in 1938 it was ruled that birth control literature was not obscene within the meaning of the legislation.

95 *Synge's ... Deirdré [of the Sorrows]*: J. M. Synge (1871–1909), Irish playwright, famous principally for plays based upon Irish peasant life, particularly in the West of Ireland. *Deirdre of the Sorrows*, unfinished when Synge died in 1909, though staged by the Abbey Theatre in 1910, was not, however, such a play. It is a tragedy drawn loosely upon Irish sagas and written in a kind of lyrical-high poetic psuedo-dialect which no longer rings true but was a style Stopes herself admired.

97 *Stetson*: Charlotte Perkins Stetson (1860–1935), better known as Charlotte Perkins Gilman. A radical American feminist, she is probably best remembered today for her short story 'The Yellow Wall-Paper' (1892).

100 *Finot*: Jean Finot (1858–1922), French sociologist. Best known in Britain for his *Race Prejudice* (1906) and *Problems of the Sexes* (1913).

102 *Tennyson*: (1809–92), Poet Laureate and perhaps the representative poet of nineteenth-century England. These lines are from his most famous poem, *In Memoriam: A.H.H.*

107 *A. C. Fifield*: Stopes's publisher.

108 *Quarterly Journal of Microscopical Science*: in the original text Stopes wrongly calls this the *Quarterly Journal Microscopical Society*.

INDEX OF NAMES AND TITLES

The Oxford World's Classics Website

www.worldsclassics.co.uk

- Information about new titles
- Explore the full range of Oxford World's Classics
- Links to other literary sites and the main OUP webpage
- Imaginative competitions, with bookish prizes
- Peruse the Oxford World's Classics Magazine
- Articles by editors
- Extracts from Introductions
- A forum for discussion and feedback on the series
- Special information for teachers and lecturers

www.worldsclassics.co.uk

American Literature

British and Irish Literature

Children's Literature

Classics and Ancient Literature

Colonial Literature

Eastern Literature

European Literature

History

Medieval Literature

Oxford English Drama

Poetry

Philosophy

Politics

Religion

The Oxford Shakespeare

A complete list of Oxford Paperbacks, including Oxford World's Classics, Oxford Shakespeare, Oxford Drama, and Oxford Paperback Reference, is available in the UK from the Academic Division Publicity Department, Oxford University Press, Great Clarendon Street, Oxford OX2 6DP.

In the USA, complete lists are available from the Paperbacks Marketing Manager, Oxford University Press, 198 Madison Avenue, New York, NY 10016.

Oxford Paperbacks are available from all good bookshops. In case of difficulty, customers in the UK can order direct from Oxford University Press Bookshop, Freepost, 116 High Street, Oxford OX1 4BR, enclosing full payment. Please add 10 per cent of published price for postage and packing.